MY MEETING WITH THE MASTERS ON MOUNT SHASTA

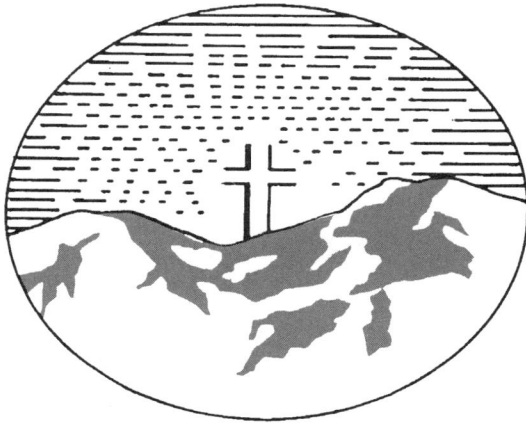

By
Nola VanValer

© Copyright 1994 by Seekers & Servers
P.O. Box 378
Mt. Shasta, CA 96067

ISBN # 0-9641571-0-1

TRIBUTE
(To Our Dear Nola)

It was in the winter of 1962 that I first met Nola Van Valer. Nola was on a lecture tour in Southern California. The particular day when I met her, she was speaking at a private residence in Lancaster, California. The audience sat spellbound, while Nola revealed her meeting with Godlike beings on the beautiful slopes of Mount Shasta in the year 1930.

She and her husband, Jerrett, had selected a little meadow beside a winding, bubbling brook surrounded with towering pines for their summer vacation campsite. One morning, one of these God-like beings walked into their camp and greeted them. In the conversation that followed, he explained that this was not a chance meeting. He told them that he had impressed Nola and Jerrett to choose this secluded spot so that he might have an opportunity to talk with them privately. For identification purposes, he told them to call him "Phylos."

Phylos explained that Mount Shasta was a magnetic field wherein he and other etheric beings of God's "angelic hosts" could return to earth and work for the enlightenment of mankind. These Great Illuminated and Unselfish Ones were known as the "Ascended Masters of Light."

Phylos explained that it is mankind's human consciousness that keeps individuals bound in their self-created limitations. In comparison, the Ascended Masters have absolute control of their lives in the way a potter controls his clay. They have earned the right to be directors of the great God Power.

The substance of the conversation with Phylos indicated that he would be pleased to teach them the truth about earthlife. Nola and Jerrett eagerly accepted his invitation. He revealed that, in the eyes of God, the campsite to which he had guided them was on holy ground. It was at this campsite that he gave them the basic foundation of spiritual unfoldment.

II.

Seeing what apt students they were, Phylos told Nola and Jerrett that it might be possible for them to come to his mountain retreat headquarters on Mount Shasta. An account of that event is portrayed within the pages of this book.

Due to this unusual meeting and the communication that continued throughout the ensuing years, Nola moved her residence to the little valley town of Mt. Shasta, California which lies at the foot of glacier-strewn Mount Shasta. Nola's new home became a sanctuary of light. She herself was like a lighted candle; her brightly burning flame ever beckoning to hungry students on the path of light. She became an Emissary through which the Ascended Masters worked and she served the people of the earth.

At the age of seventy-six, Nola became the publisher of the "Friendly Letter Service," a monthly publication. This free letter reached out into thirty-four foreign countries. It assisted students of light to face their life experiences with common sense reasoning. The "Friendly Letter Service" was a phenomenal success.

In the autumn of her life, Nola bloomed like a rose and consequently expanded her workload. She founded a nonprofit organization which she named the Radiant School. For some years, the Radiant School lessons were a great blessing to seekers living in isolated and remote places and put them in touch with God's word. With the help of a few loyal students, Nola accomplished all this work in her own home. She never accepted any money for her personal needs.

Strangers who came to Nola's door were always warmly welcomed. Those whose journey was long were invited to stay for dinner. After dinner, the group would assemble in her large living room to hear about Phylos and his words of wisdom. Many who met Nola had their lives improved beyond belief through their association with her.

As the years passed, Nola was confined to a wheel chair as the result of an injury received during World War II.

Even when she was suffering much pain, she continued to teach students. When she finally became bed-ridden, she would still see one student at a time. At other times, several students would gather around her bed to receive instructions.

Our beloved Nola lived to the ripe old age of ninety-two years. She passed from physical life on May 22, 1979. Needless to say, her spirit of love lived on in the hearts of her students. Nola could not be forgotten by anyone who met her.

The above has been submitted by a student so athirst for the naked truth that, after meeting Nola in Lancaster, he moved to Mt. Shasta and studied under her for many years. This student was present when Nola gave her last lesson five days before her death. In his close association with her, he had the opportunity to absorb Nola's down-to-earth brand of Christian philosophy based upon the expression of Divine Love, the most powerful force in the universe, precisely as Phylos had been instructed to teach her by Our Savior, the Lord Jesus Christ.

The material for this book was taped by Nola in the years before her death in preparation for the writing of her own book. She had planned it as a sequel to her little booklet, "Tramp at My Door." However, her loyal devotion to her work and her students prevented the time to do this. Now her wish has been granted in memorandum and with great love and with the hope that this book will touch the hearts of those who read it.

Kenneth Wheeler, Phd, D.D.

TABLE OF CONTENTS

CHAPTER I

OUR COMING TO MT. SHASTA

I will begin by telling about how I first heard of Mt. Shasta. I was from the East and a newcomer to California. All I knew of the mountains was what I learned in geography at school. I had never seen the mountains; it was only a word to me.

My husband, Jerry, was returning from the East to our home in San Jose with decisions from the medical profession that he had incurable heart trouble. On the platform of the railway station in Salt Lake City, he met a man who, in appearance, was like a Greek priest. This man had on a long black robe, a high hat, a long black beaded chain around his neck with a large cross at the end, and wore a heavy beard. This strange priest approached Jerry and told him that because of trouble with heavy snow and rain it was not possible to continue on through to Nevada and then California, but that if he could get on a train to Portland he could then take the Shasta Limited to California and arrive home just one day later. Jerry was astonished when this priest told him they could not get through because of snowslides, of which there had been several, which had to be cleared before the train could continue, and that this would delay them about twenty-four hours. The priest told Jerry to go and ask the station master and that he would tell him that the train to Portland would leave within the hour. Jerry went into the station and questioned the station master as to the delay regarding his train and the possibility of traveling on the train soon to leave for Portland. The station master confirmed what the priest had told Jerry and told him, "Yes, I can arrange for you to go on the other route into Portland and from there you will come down through California to your destination. You will be delayed only a few hours from your original arrival time and have all the accomodations on the Northwestern Railway that you had on the Western Pacific."

Jerry decided to make the change and continue home, believing that his wife would be worrying about him. Strangely enough, when he got on the train to Portland and went to his assigned car and seat, the "Greek priest," as Jerry thought of him, was sitting in the seat across from him. The priest began to talk to Jerry and told him that, when they passed through Northern California, they would see Mount Shasta, the most beautiful mountain in the world and Jerry told him that he had never seen it before. The priest went on to say that the town of Mt. Shasta, situated just at the bottom of the mountain, was a very unusual place and that there was much unexplained phenomena surrounding Mount Shasta itself. He told Jerry of strange lights that many people saw on the mountain and that even train passengers often saw strange occurrences as they passed.

The priest told him of a miraculous light which had been the cause of preventing a serious train wreck only a short time before. He sensed Jerry's questioning of these things and called the train conductor to verify the incident of the miraculous light. The conductor told Jerry that on the very train he was now riding and just a short time previously, the engineer saw a blinding light, could not see and had to stop the train. When the train was stopped, the light disappeared and the engineer saw that there was a huge boulder on the tracks just a few feet in front of the train. Had the train not stopped just when it did, there would have been a fatal accident as the train would have hit the boulder and surely have plunged over the steep cliff.

Jerry then listened to many other strange things of which the priest told him and he could sense the truth that might be in them. The priest then amazed Jerry by telling him that he knew of his heart problem and that he could be healed by the priest's elder brother. Having a Christian Science background, Jerry knew healings of this kind were at least possible. As they talked, Jerry began to believe that maybe this priest and his elder brother could help him. The priest told Jerry that if he would make a short stop at the Mt. Shasta Railway Station, he would see to it that Jerry received help.

Jerry was hesitant when they arrived at Mt. Shasta but thought he would step out on the platform for a minute and think about what to do about all he had heard.

Jerry told me:

"When I got off the train, I did not have my coat or hat, for I expected to be off of the train for only a few minutes. Parked and waiting at the station was a wonderful, large limosine complete with chauffer. I had never seen anything so beautiful and thought only great and wealthy men could have such an expensive looking automobile."

"The priest was at my side and took me over to the limosine. The chauffer said, 'enter, we are waiting,' and the priest and I got into the limosine and were then driven over a road used by logging trucks (no smooth highway as exists today). We were driven to McCloud (a town about fifteen miles from Mt. Shasta that is nestled at the bottom of the other side of Mount Shasta) and drove into the only service station in that town. I was asked if I would like to go to the men's room and I did. When I came out, there was no limosine, no chauffer, and no priest, but there was another man, a white horse, and a track cart of an ancient make, wherein the passenger lifted up the seat to get in beside the driver. I was asked to get into the cart and was informed that I would be traveling in this manner for some time.

"I had no coat or hat and was wondering if I had lost my mind. We traveled for about eight miles, evening approached and we then crossed over a stream and through a gate. We had had no trouble with snow on the roads. Inside the gate was a Chinese-styled home which was surrounded by a porch. I did not feel cold and the evening was clear and the sky filled with stars.

"I entered into the home, which was tastefully decorated and had a strange fireplace which opened into three parts of it. I was told to sit down and rest and was served with food. The meal was a Chinese creation with strange vegetables and a clear liquid soup. The soup was wonderful and was served with a hard biscuit. The man who served it was Chinese and he told me that I could call him Mol Long. Strange as it may seem, I felt I knew this man. He then told me to relax for awhile and then I would continue on to meet the priest's elder brother.

"For how long I rested, I do not know, but, as I did so, I looked around and observed my surroundings. There was a beautiful clock table and a massive chair and table. When I accidently touched the table, it moved so easily

3

that it was almost weightless."

"When I was told that I would now continue my journey, I went outside expecting to find the cart and horse but was told we would now be traveling by foot. Mol Long guided us as we began to walk. There I was, in army-type shoes, a light suit, and with no coat or hat. I thought to myself, 'Jerry, you will freeze to death and no on will ever find your body until Spring.' It was too late for me to turn back now, after coming all this way, and we continued on until we came to a place with a spring. Mol Long told me that I was to rest and that this was holy ground at the spring. There was a fire that felt very warm and I thought to myself that I must have been cold and still I did not ever feel cold.

"Mol Long took a thin, large handkerchief from his pocket, through which the fire glowed. He placed it upon the ground and told me to sit upon it and then produced from somewhere a bowl with clear soup which tasted like nothing I have ever tasted upon this earth. I drank the soup and became so alive with vibration that I was at complete peace and rest within myself, and had no care for anything. Then Mol Long took another handkerchief and told me to take off my shoes to rest my feet, after which he placed over me the other sheet. I could not have been warmer and yet had only one sheet beneath me and one sheet on top of me. He then told me to rest and sleep and that he would watch over me. I watched this Chinaman in his pose of meditation until I fell asleep.

"I knew not how long I slept until Mol Long awakened me and told me it was time to go to meet the elder brother. I was unwashed and unshaven but felt fresh and clean. Although I did not feel hungry, I was given a bowl of warm liquid and, after drinking it, seemed to be filled with strength. I followed Mol Long up a path, a Forest Service path, for about a half a mile, until we came into the open where the moonlight displayed the many beautiful trees that glistened all around beneath us like a fairyland. There were objects that looked like glowing lights on the mountain. It was beautiful! Under three great trees, the moonlight cast a shadow on the snow and, approaching from about a hundred yards away, was a being I thought must be God. The illumination was so great around him that no light I had ever seen could be

4

compared. The light seemed to be everywhere; all-glistening in the quietness and beauty of the mountain.

"As the being approached, he stopped twenty feet from me and said, 'Come to me, my son, child of earth. You have a pure mind and therefore God has a use for you. Your heart will not bother you, as it is healed insofar as your physical body is concerned, and will not hinder your pattern that is to be fulfilled. We desire you to go home and prepare to come back to this mountain with your wife and stay for the month of June of this year and we will teach you. There are no mysteries of the mountain but many truths you can find and know. Prepare for warm weather.'

"I felt as though a hand were placed upon my head and I was thanking God that I had been privileged to stand before this great being. I prayed He would bless me and give me the strength to fulfill whatever it was that I was to do. I opened my eyes, which I had closed, and the being was gone. Mol Long told me it was time to return to the train station. There was no darkness; it seemed to be very light."

"I cannot tell you how long it took us to return to Mol Long's home. There I waited for the cart and horse and then the driver and I continued back down the old road, over rushing water and bumps, until we arrived once again in McCloud. There was snow everywhere. I saw no people and, when we arrived at the service station, there was the limosine and chauffer, and I was driven to the train station. I thought that my trip since leaving the station had taken twenty-four hours and that I would be meeting the train that would be coming the next evening. To my surprise, it was the same train from which I had departed only twenty minutes before at the Mt. Shasta depot. I did not know how this had happened but I do know that it happened.

"I got back on the train to continue my journey but the priest was no longer there. I spoke to no one on the trip home. The train arrived at the Oakland station. I rode the ferry across the bay and got on the final train of my homeward trip. Many thoughts were in my mind and I was anxious to arrive at home. You, my dear wife, met me in San Jose and were not surprised I was late. You showed me the telegram you had received, telling me I had

5

nothing to explain, which told you of my detour. I do not know who sent you the telegram; I only know it was sent."

We immediately began to make plans and preparations to go to Mt. Shasta in June. We left San Jose on May 27, 1930.

Jerry's nephew, Bill, and his wife, Leona, and their two young nieces, Myrtle and Lucille, came along with us on our mountain adventure. We went directly to McCloud and from there were told which way to go to arrive at the pure spring, the same spring where Jerry had had his healing experience. This was the first camping trip to the wilderness for any of us and we spent a few days setting up a proper camp and adjusting to camp life. We all wondered what experiences lay ahead of us at this blessed place. Every day, each of us would have a turn at directing our exploration and we would all go off together to discover the beauties of Mount Shasta.

After lunch on June 5th, we decided we would follow Lucille's direction and, after a fifteen-minute meditation, we started out across a ravine through the manzanita toward the tall trees. We thought we might be able to see Mount Shasta without climbing as far this time as we had been. We had gone through about one-half mile of manzinita so dense, that I never would have believed humans could have possibly done so, when we arrived at a large stone. It was massive, about twelve feet high and the sides went up straight. We walked all around the stone and, of course, we all wanted to climb up to the top. We helped each other to climb up to the top of the rock. Once there, we still could not see over the trees which veiled Mount Shasta. We sat on the top of the rock for about a half an hour, talking about our adventure, and, just as we were going to leave, Jerry decided we should give thanks to Our Heavenly Father for the opportunity of being there, his wonderful health, and the peace and quietness of the mountain. We stood in a circle and joined hands and, after Jerry prayed and said, "Amen," he asked us all to express in turn and we did.

At that moment, as the last one of us had finished, the rock began to move and quiver with some great power similar to an earthquake. A mighty voice came from the direction of our camp and said:

"Beloved Children of Earth, the God-power that is

6

stronger than man has brought you here. I am a voice from the God-realm. We have invited you here to teach you the laws given to all you children of earth to use divinely and rightly. There is nothing mysterious. There is no endowment of power on any one particular person. None are chosen except that they choose to serve in truth and light. You have had your days of rest and, if now you will permit the time and opportunity to learn, God will send you the angel to teach you so that you may serve your fellowman on earth.

"We take from you nothing, we require of you no obligation, vows, or promises. We ask you to adjust your life and its program for a little time, of learning how to think in a different manner so that you may see clearly and with understanding. God's laws work today upon the earth as they did when Jesus Christ walked upon the earth. I am Phylos, the Tibetan. I was Zalim, the man of Atlantis. I am a high priest in the Great White Brotherhood Melchizedek Order. My voice comes from the Temple on Mount Shasta. If you will arrange to meet us at the three trees where you go to view the valley, we will teach you there."

"It was the power of the Heavenly force that you felt through the mineral rock that you stand upon. When you return to your camp, have a moderate evening meal, preferably of vegetables, and be finished so you may have a wonderful campfire tonight. The sky will be clear and the moon will shine to give you a vision we have planned for your evening. Talk it over. We make you give no obligation or promise, only that you do what you intend to do."

The voice was silent. We stood for a time; our hands still clasped together. It was strange how different parts of the message had affected each one of us. We got down off the rock and when all were safely down, returned to camp.

No one talked on the way back or after we had returned. We quietly prepared and ate supper and held our usual evening service. It was our custom to hold a song service. We sang hymns and sacred songs and other songs that we enjoyed singing together. At 8:30 p.m., we always had our healing silence. On this evening of June 5, 1930, we had gone into silence as usual after our singing and had been in meditation for about five

7

minutes when Lucille squeezed my hand. I opened my eyes and saw that she and Jerry were pointing at twenty-eight deer. They were all looking toward the fire with eyes shining and they watched us in silence.

As we were watching the deer, we heard a wonderful chorus of voices approaching until we could see forms coming towards us. There were more than we could count; a multitude. They were in blue and grey robes and were led by the twelve white robed beings. They stopped in front of us and the twelve talked to us and told us of the Temple on Mt. Shasta, that many had entered there and that we were also being prepared to come and enter into the Temple. The twelve talked to us for about ten minutes. We were told that if we would place ourselves in their hands for teaching, we would be given reasonable words that we would be able to understand for our learning. We were also told how it would be accomplished that from the third dimension we would be able to function in the fourth dimension in both body and mind. All that was required of us was that we conduct our camp life a little higher as to our method of thinking, and that we should come to the three trees for further instruction on June 7th. The decision we chose to make would be up to each one of us.

The fire became like a rainbow and a flame issued forth from a log. When it had died down, all the beings retired to whence they had come. Their singing was like a chanting and was filled with great joy. We were requested to retire from the fireside, to do no talking, and to think over well all that we had heard and seen. To say that we were excited and emotional was to say the least, but we could not talk so we went quietly to bed, determined to think about what our individual choice would be.

By morning, Jerry and I had made our choice to listen and be taught and to do our best to follow the truths about which we would learn. From that point, we all met the Master each day at a spot known to us as "three trees." It was at the very same spot that Jerry had been healed of his heart condition by Jesus the Christ earlier in the Spring and where the three trees stood in a triangle. For us, it was a holy place; the place where each of us had a blessed experience wherein we were privileged to meet the Masters from the Radiant Temple on Mount Shasta.

We arrived at the three trees on that first day full of joy and anticipation, not knowing exactly what to expect. We closed our eyes and meditated for some time in order to calm ourselves and be ready for whatever was to happen. Upon opening our eyes, we beheld a most remarkable being. I saw him standing by a tree; a most beautiful being dressed in a white robe with a gold cloth on his head and another around his waist. Part of this cloth was tossed over his shoulder and the other end was almost to the end of the hem of his robe. He stood there and his face held a most beautiful smile; his eyes were shining with a light which I cannot explain but he looked as though he understood our very thoughts. I touched Jerry and birds burst into song as I had never heard them sing before. Then a light began to extend out from this being until it was almost touching us. He lifted his hand, his right hand, and said:

"Greetings, Children of Earth. My soul greets thee. My heart is filled with love for all fellowman. I will speak words of truth from these lips and give praise to God on High."

He seemed not to be in a hurry and expressed to us perfect calmness. We all felt at peace. It did not seem to disturb him that all of us were there. We all sensed that he had expected it to be so. He told us that he would talk to us in general because we each were on a different pattern of life and that he would say his words so that all would understand.

Following are a small measure of the truths that he taught to us at the three trees on Mount Shasta. If these teachings of truth touch your heart, I ask you to explore more deeply within yourself. If you choose to do so, I will indeed feel blessed.

He then continued by saying:

"Children, you are the earth product. Many of the earth family blame the world for its conditions but they need go no furher than themselves. Every man is responsible for the conditions on the earth. Man should not blame their religious beliefs, for, if they live their religious beliefs, they will be a Christian at heart. The attitude of the American people towards their religious tendencies are that they should still them instead of awakening them. So, we advise all of you to study more about what

9

your intentions are regarding religion so that you may apply them and not tell others how to use theirs. We advise you to keep your minds high above destruction and pray continually for peace. For if a man thinketh thus, he lends his power of thought to overcome evil.

"Where two or more of you are joined together, if you spend one moment in gratefulness for protection of all people, it will help. I shall give to you the things of thought in spiritual words that will help you to unfold your understanding that you may live with the light, walk in the light, and use the light that Jesus the Christ used on earth. When I ask you to bring your book of holy words with you, I will refer to many parts of your bible and show you how you have misused the words that you thought were good English teachings. I am sure that those of you who have attended church programs have heard that God created you and all the other earthly beings. That He did create this planet; its mineral kingdoms, animal and plant kingdom, and all kingdoms you know. You know little of what He created above or below. He did not create this physical body of yours; He created the substance of which it was made. Many believe that this is the only body of you and yet, you say, there is a spirit of you that lives after death. Your physical body is only a small fraction of you. I shall teach you of other bodies, and every part of you of which I shall teach you is spoken of in your holy book."

"As it is written, it is true, for those who wrote the book were inspired by the masters above, such as Jesus your Christ, who knew the words to be as they really and truly are for understanding. Do not sit in judgment that what you are learning is the only path on which to travel. Every religion, every group of students who join together, are on a path and they can only go as high as their ability to understand will take them. This is not because the teacher does not teach them well, not because their belief is placed in the wrong direction; it is because they cannot rise to understand what is being taught. This is the reason there is so much discontent throughout the churches; throughout the religious organizations. People become so solemn over something they do not understand and this is what causes the discontent."

"If you have heard about hell as preached from the

pulpits, this is only a misinterpretation as its meaning is changed out of fear. There is no burning hell and much torture for those who do not live a certain type of life. This is only a misinterpretation. There is no burning hell; not as we know burning upon this earth. There is a hell but the word "hell" is not interpreted as you know it, as a pit. Hell is your own conscience, both in the physical life and in the invisible spiritual life of you. The physical life and the spiritual life is what forms your pattern of life that you, in the flesh, must carry out. If you have hated in a physical life and you are reborn on earth (Oh yes, children, it is true that when you pass into spirit-land through the change that is called death, you learn of the failures of your life on earth and come back reborn, incarnated into a being of flesh again.), you are born again to work out the hate that you had lived before."

"Now the difference in me as I stand before you is that I lived many lives upon the earth and I descended to the earth from a kingdom that was not the man kingdom but was a being kingdom known as the Elohim, or Sons of God. I descended to earth to teach. I was a high priest in those days that I lived on earth and there were no colleges or professors of education. The high priests were the only ones that were considered to be of the educated class of people. When I came to earth as a divine being, I took on flesh and I found how sweet the passions of earth were. I found how delirious one can become with power and how unbalanced one can become with education. Eventually, I was so enmeshed in the evils of earth that I was similar to all others born on earth. When I became useless of body, I too entered spirit-land by death and there I saw how I had made so many mistakes. It matters not whether you call it hatred, enmity, jealousy, anger, lust, passion; the price to be paid is the same. I had to be reborn in flesh again and again and again; three generations did I pass through until I found my freedom by overcoming death, by not entering again into spirit-land but ascending into the home kingdom from whence I had descended to earth.

"The masters of the group of which I am now serving were known as the fallen angels. It is not man on earth that is the fallen angel, it is those of the master kingdom; the Elohim or Sons of God who visited the earth among men and became known as the fallen angels. I ascended back into the body, the life-body that was given to me in the beginning. It appears to you of flesh, but it is not the flesh of earth; it is the substance of flesh in its purest state. It can be both visible and invisible but it is not the spirit body. A spirit body is known as the physical substance body of your flesh body, often referred to as the ghost body. So I appear to you, not as a spirit and not as a ghost, but as a manifestation of the God body.

"Yes, we appear to many. There are many of us who come to the earth to help every race of man. I have been sent to this place. I am here to save the American man and am one of many who are all over the United States, Canada, and even South America. We are designated to save the portion of those races that can be purified. You have not been chosen because you are you, but through some past event you have earned the right to know the truth that you might be set free. You shall meet the Masters of the Temple on Mt. Shasta. We cannot tell you just when it will be. You will go by your own efforts of your physical body up onto the mountain and there meet the Masters. There are twelve in the counsil, although at certain times there are thirteen. You shall learn about them all. You shall learn about the angels that God has given to be in charge over you. You shall know them and they will assist your efforts of truth and light towards your heavenly life. I will greet you on your next day. I am blessing each of you, that your day shall be one of peace and that every moment of your stay on this mountain shall be in your consciousness for all your life. Amen, Amen, Amen.

FOLLOWING ARE THE WORDS SPOKEN BY THIS BEING IN HIS TEACHING OF TRUTH AND LIGHT.

CHAPTER II

THE KINGDOMS OF HEAVEN AND EARTH

Beloved Children of Earth, may every step of your path of light bring you peace and joy and may your fountain of life be filled with the waters that purify. I give you the greetings of the Great White Brotherhood. My soul greets thee. My heart is filled with love for all fellowman. I shall speak words of truth, giving praise to God on High. Amen, amen, amen.

Children of Light, I am sure you feel the responsibility of keeping in memory the words that I give to you and of which you shall hear for many years coming. I will tell you that this is not a program as in a school. There is nothing that you can sell that is of the truth because it belongs to everyone. If you seek to profit from this truth, you are deceiving the heart of man.

I shall tell you this day the meaning of the word 'master' of which we prefer you to use in our instance instead of 'spirit guide' or 'angel,' because there is much difference in those words and to use them without giving the true meaning is another way of misleading in false understanding. I advise you that when you can find a book that will give to you the understanding of the words God, Lord God, Lord, Heavenly Father, Father, Archangel, Master and Angels, with the study of kingdom, dimension, earth and universe, then study them. When you have these words so that you can form the understanding of those who will be speaking to you about them, you are well on a path of light. Without this understanding or foundation, you are incapable of understanding what others are understanding and endeavoring to explain to you.

Now, if you do not know what the meaning of a universe is, then you will have to take these words and make every effort to find, in completeness, a modern use of these words so that you may form a true understanding. First, you must realize that your kingdom is only part of a space of your universe. Let us look at the earth as a small ball that you hold in your hand. If you desire to have it down in measurements that you can understand, we will say that the ball is four inches through from east to west and north to south points. That would make your universe measure four inches for each of these realms or regions that we call kingdoms. Around your earth is a four inch belt, or around this ball that is claiming to be earth, is a four inch space belt that you call your atmosphere and around that is another four inch belt that you call your dense ether. Around that belt is another four inch belt that you call your light ether, around that belt is another belt that you call your rarified ether and around that belt is the purest ether known. It is the space ether of your universe and this is your limitation of your earth universe. There are many great spaces where many other universes are, in their evolution, also. Now, these spaces that I am giving to you are like dimensions. In each of these spaces, you can only work with the body that will work in that space. There is but one way you can reach into this space and that is with your God-mind.

Now, I have drawn a picture for you to hold above your earth-thinking that you may know in what direction we are referring when I speak of the kingdoms. So likewise, this space that you call your earth-universe is divided into twelve divisions that are called kingdoms. They are not your ether space, not the ethereal-cosmic ether, but they are made as to regions in space. They do not have up and down or east and west. They do not go in circles and you will not be able to understand that as yet, so do not let that disturb you. I am trying to get you to picture that there are twelve different spaces that are called kingdoms.

The first beings that were created and placed in the first highest kingdom were the gods that rule this earth. I am sorry to impose upon you that you are misunderstanding if you believe that there is but one god created to rule this earth, for Almighty God placed twelve gods in these kingdoms and they rule the earth, or the earth universe. Their first creations were the Lord Gods and they were in the second kingdom. In the third kingdom that was created, where the word 'Lord' means thousands or law, it has no limitations, for they are the ones that rule by power in your universe. Without them, there is disorder

14

and confusion. Now all this takes place out into space from which no man in a living, physical body can find.

In your fourth kingdom are the Arch-angels. They are the ones that build all patterns of everything that is in your earth and on your earth; everything that is in the air above you that you call your life.

Your next kingdom in space contains those that are called the Heavenly Fathers and there are thousands of Heavenly Fathers, each to its own race and tribe. Their duties I will tell you about before you leave this portion of the country. All of these kingdoms are what is called or known as natural power and no earth force ever has any power to rule over them.

Your next kingdom has the creation of that which is through your dense ether to the earth and is known as the Father Kingdom; not your parent father but the Father of all nature in every kingdom from here down. He works with the energies of the earth.

Your next division is the Sons of God; the kingdom of the Sons of God or Elohim. They are the first creation of soul life. Here you find the first division of mind/God mind. In the soul life, there is but the God mind; there is no lower mind.

Your next division is the kingdom of the angels. Now these angels are not the same as your Arch-angels. They are the angels divided into many divisions that work in the space upon the earth and in the earth. Many of the stories that are told, which you would call myths and mysteries that include the many names of the visible and invisible; fairies, elves, gnomes and many other divisions, even to brownies, are in the divisions of the angels. They are the workers that produce nature upon your earth. But there is also a division that are called the muses and I would advise many of you to look up and ponder over the division of the muses, for they work with your mental intelligence, your capacity of doing, your limitations and, what is best, they work with how to develop your intelligence, which includes your five physical senses and leads you to the higher mind/God mind, which has its divisions of which I shall call, at this time, the twelve disciples.

Then, my Children of Light, you come to your kingdom of mortal beings. They are the first beings created

upon earth to take on their shapes in either one of the four bodies of which I shall tell you.

Your next division of kingdom is the human kingdom. The next is the plant kingdom and the last is the mineral kingdom.

Now I see the question of how I left out the animal kingdom, but I have not left it out and I will now tell you why. In your mineral kingdom, of which is best for students to begin with, the first kingdom is number one. The last kingdom of which we began shall be known as the twelfth kingdom. It was not the first one but the last as they come down. Now, as you go up, we will take mineral as number one created and it is divided into seven planes and you will find classifications for everything that is in rock, soil, and water. Just as you find by chemical tests, you can have liquid compounds or powers, so likewise it is in the mineral kingdom.

Your second kingdom, which is the plant, I am sure you can see as you look out over this valley. You can see as many as seven different divisions of the plant kingdom; the vegetable kingdom.

As you look out over the next kingdom, it means anything that has intelligence of any degree whatsoever that reproduces its kind. This includes, by seven planes, the fowl of the air, fish of the sea, reptiles, the beasts of the fields and all animals in their classifications, each to his own kind as you have cattle and other animals divided. So likewise is each kingdom divided and over all of these, in each of its many divisions in its seven different planes of life, are seven different oversouls, each ruling its own kind. There is no other life than the dying of the old and the taking on of the new until they have built a body where their own individual intelligence of mind, mental mind, takes over. I hope you ponder over this quite a spell, until you can see and picture that of which I am telling you.

In the next kingdom comes the mortal man and in the mortal man's kingdom is the first kingdom of the beings. If you are capable of understanding how there are seven planes in each kingdom, then you will understand that there are seven different divisions, beginning with the lowest who have only the instinct of nature. These are the animal kingdom. They are capable of using their mental intelligence by finding out for what things are meant, such as to touch heat means to burn; to touch cold means chill and so forth. Until they can develop their intelligence, they cannot go any higher. In your next division, you have man, who has begun to use his own mental intelligence and is on the road or path whereby he makes his own evolution. He does not have an oversoul; he has an individual direction. He knows nothing else except his flesh body and the satisfaction of its work. In your third division, you still have man as a being and he begins his classification as an individual; one who is capable of thinking for himself; one who is capable of finding conclusions by reasoning.

In your fourth division of man's mortal kingdom, you find the individual man who has become magnetically tuned to his higher self. It is then that he is given in charge of his angel who guards him in the rest of his time in his earth lives. This pattern begins the evolution of his **mortal** being. It is his first awakening that, when he dies, he does not go into hell or heaven but into a space that belongs to your earth kingdom. There he is taught how to make another earth body out of the substance that is also a physical substance that he alone cannot understand. He also is given a master, of whom I shall teach you of what it means, who takes charge of his pattern which he takes into earth life with him.

There he must work out his own pattern until he finds his higher self.

Then he goes into his next pattern, which is his fifth pattern. This is the pattern where he takes on responsibility for his family tree; his earth branches of life where he sets aside that which he has learned as lessons well taken care of and that which he has not learned by his stubbornness of his lower will of self-rule called karma, sin, or error. Then man is given the opportunity to take on his next self, which is the workings of knowing all that is out away from man; that which he calls his heavens; that which he calls his higher natures; that which he calls his God mind. That is what is meant by the two divisions being joined together. If he can find great pleasure in seeking not only that which is within but that which is without, he will find many helpers to take him on the path upward. He may eventually get away from the earth to which he is tied by bondage.

In the last step of his mortal human existence, man has the opportunity to live as man perfected in his higher self. He has his own decision to make. Shall he become the Son of God, to overcome death, or shall he long to indulge his life always upon earth? In these decisions, man has with him not only the guardian angel who has charge of the pattern of each individual but, added to him, he is given the helpers of the masters who will keep him away from those things that would drive him back to earth. You are not capable of understanding how there are so many types of forces, so much magnetic attraction that man, even though he has perfected, unto his last day he can be dragged back into earth's fold; earth's limitations, and, once he steps down, he must work his way back up.

Now the answer, after you have reached the seventh division of your kingdom, is: If you go into spirit-land when you pass out of your physical body, you must be reborn again, unless you are capable of being taught and you, like many there, dedicate your soul to salvation; until those you have left behind who you have ever in any way misled or have thoughtlessly harmed, or have caused them heartaches or pain, are brought through, you do not ascend. Now let us say again the last words that your great teacher on earth gave you: "The last enemy that you shall overcome is death." When you are capable of passing from your physical body with no desire of ever returning to it and your mind is capable of understanding the earth and the heavens, you are ready to ascend, as did Jesus, the man you claimed the greatest savior of man, the Son of God.

I want you, on my last words, to consider that you have, in your kingdom of man, your seven divisions of evolution. You never evolved from a pollywog or could you ever blame man's evolution on a monkey. God created each kingdom to its own evolution and God's universe has a perfection for each one of the kingdoms. He does not need to take one type to make another. Now, of your seven planes in your kingdom, in each one of those planes there are seven divisions and in your bible, where it refers to 7-7-7, this is the meaning of it.   Amen, Amen, Amen.

CHAPTER III

EXPLANATION OF ASCENSION

On this mother earth before me, I can see the light in your eyes; the astonishment and wonder of the words I have said; but every word, my Children of Earth, is true. When your Beloved Savior said the Father in me and the Father in you are the same, I say to you, that God in you and God in me are the same. You, likewise, are the Son of God. You, likewise, will some day ascend as I ascended. When you walk with God, you are no more. The bible is filled with truths and you cannot afford to pass them by. I will explain to you some of the great teachings, that you may follow more attentively and find a deep understanding.

I come to teach you the things of earth; not to cover them with mystery but to reveal to you the cause and effect of each life that is lived upon the earth, from the ages gone by to the present time. All is intended for the perfection of man on earth.

You have read the story that was compiled that is now the book called "Dweller on Two Planets."* I will tell you the reason why I have given it. In the first part of the book, I endeavored to explain how, in the ages past, man was created almost in perfection by knowing his own God-self and the uses of the invisible side of life. I then endeavored to show to you the experiences I passed through as the man Zailm. He had every available pattern to live out in truth and the fullness of life, until he could ascend back to where he was in perfection, a Son of God. But because of temptation, the physical desires were greater than his spiritual qualities. He found that he would have to live many lives; that is, the returning to the back and forth of death until he could erase all intentional acts of sin or error. I endeavored to show you how God never neglects his children and to reveal the truth of what

*" Dweller on Two Planets" by Phylos is available through several sources in any metaphysical bookstore.

19

is called the 'sinful' way and what is termed the 'spiritual' way of living. For man does have a choice; it is his own choice that leads him up or down; that hinders and retards his progression, or, if he takes advantage, can speed his time to perfection. I did not give the first writing in the book for amusement; I gave it as a program to understand your life's problems or pattern. I did not cover the lives that were in between the time of Atlantis until the time that I came as Walter Pierson. There was much that came between as the years passed by; as the lives came and I ascended into spirit-land. I only covered those that are most important, that you may be able to guide your own life's pattern with understanding of cause and effect.

Now I am going to give to you the reason why I am still attached to earth. When I descended as a Son of God to this earth, I had not tasted of the physical life and, because I came in contact with those lives upon earth that I had not been accustomed to in my heavenly abode, I became enmeshed in sinful ways of desires and harm to those that lived on earth as flesh men. And when I did pass away from my first earth existence in a flesh body, I entered into a strange land where I found many, many who had lived upon earth who were waiting for an opportunity to return to earth, for they said, "Until you return to earth and undo and make good the things you left undone or the things you committed an error in doing, you cannot ever get out of spirit-land." A short time after passing into this spirit-land, a great, shining being came and said to me, "I shall teach you how to return to earth whereby you can correct your errors and bring peace to those that you have harmed. When you have found the way to make right all these things you know in your heart were not right, then I will help you once again to ascend into that place you call your abode, the Kingdom of the Masters. I am likened to a guardian angel. I will go back to earth with you and I will endeavor to guide you to fulfill the pattern that you must take upon your shoulders. It is the yoke that you must pick up and carry as your burden. You must rest awhile and, in that rest, we will help you gather together enough material, the substance of flesh, to make another body and you must take on the flesh-body and be born through a mother's womb, because you are not the ascended master now; you are a man of the mortal being tribe"

I do not know how long I slept; I do not know how long I stayed in spirit-land, but while there, I was given great knowledge and understanding of how they teach on the other side to those who make many failures in their lives. I was taught how many times you continued back and forth in your death body and then in your life body and always there were those of the Great Kingdom of the Angels who taught and helped each one, that they may be a different type when they go back to earth. I was told that when I returned to earth, I might not have wealth at my command; neither would I find the loving parents that some other children would have when they come to earth. My life would be hard to bear but that was the way that I would be able to undo much that I left behind on earth.

So, it took many years. I did not count them because only certain lives stand out in anyone's pattern to show the progress that is made. I eventually arrived back to the grounds upon which I had stood with its great mountain peaks and placed in records as the history of the lost Atlantis. I was there to recount again. I was there to be shown again that I, in some way, must bring forth those records for the good of mankind.

In one particular life that I lived on earth, I knew that in some coming, future time (for this was about the time that your Savior walked upon the earth) I would work again upon the earth as a leader of light. I knew and recognized that Son of Light, that Teacher of all Teachers, that greatest of all healers and knew him to be my elder brother and that I again must, like He, work on earth. So, each life that I had in between the time of Zailm and that which you know as Phylos, I came back many times to this mountain that you call Mount Shasta.

Now I shall explain that I, whom you knew as Zalim and now you recognize as Phylos and yet you do not know me because the word 'Phylos' designates a high priest of the Melchizedek Order of the Great White Brotherhood, do not have an earth name. You would not understand that we do not go by names in the Kingdom of the Masters. There are teachers all over your earth that have been, in the past, recognized as great leaders in your past. They are all high priests; they are Phylos. So, when you speak of me, you are referring to me as high priest; one who teaches truth.

In my last life as Walter Pierson, I did not at first know why I was so attracted to Mount Shasta. But I soon learned that I could not live unless I fathomed the truth of why I was so attracted to this great mountain. Yes, I made acquaintances. I did not know that everyone with whom I made contact, I had been in contact with many times in many lives and especially on the continent of Atlantis. Here we had gathered together to rise above material life or be enmeshed in many more lives. I gave the words to one who was very sensitive to the high spiritual vibrations of the fourth dimension. Because I had known him in the previous lives many times, I was able to communicate to him and give to him in writing the story that you read as "Dweller on Two Planets." No, he did not write upon the mountain the story that you read as a book. He has been on the mountain in his physical body as a young man and he has been there many times in his spiritual existence of life. The effort was in putting out the work. The physical mind could not write the things of the fourth dimension; the changing of the bodies. They did not have the ability to explain that life went from one kingdom to another in ascension and so it was necessary to give to him strange words and actions and let him put them together to the best of his ability. The reason was that, if we could get ten or one thousand to read the words, it would be the egg that would hatch results of spiritual teaching by truths of ascension.

I will assure you that, when that young man had finished, his life work was finished. He no more has to live upon the earth. He no more has to pass away by death; he has earned his freedom. As Walter Pierson, I also earned freedom. I could have ascended into the kingdom away from the earth but, in my first mission being sent upon the earth to teach the truth, I found I had failed and now I desired to take up the work again. So I was blessed by the great leaders of the Melchizedek Order with my mission back on earth. I have worked and made plans that I may be able to call together many to learn of the truth. I have called them to the mountain, because the mountain is filled with the light of the fourth dimension and there we are able to pass it out, as it were, until the bodies are prepared to be accustomed to live in and with the fourth dimension. This is necessary for the mind to accept; the night side of life to that which you call your physical manifestation.

Now, enough of my life except to tell you that, when you were born in the beginning from a divine body into a flesh body, you were given a pattern and in that pattern was the effect of every life you lived. I tell you that you have lived many lives in flesh bodies upon this earth, even before the time mentioned in Atlantis, and that you are today walking the earth seeking a freedom to become the enlightened Children of God. I could not tell you that God has chosen certain ones upon the earth because to say those words would not reveal the truth. All the children on earth are Children of God. You must remember the word 'God' means many. There are many gods and many gods have created. When I say that all in the kingdom of the mineral kind were created by God, that is true, but that god did not create the human man. When I say there are gods that created the plant or vegetable kingdom, I do not say that is the god that created man, and so on in kingdom to kingdom, man to man. There are great changes and many gods. Until you learn of it all, it is a mixed-up pattern because your mental mind is not capable of accepting outside of a certain limit that you call your intelligence.

It will be my endeavor to help you find a way to enlighten your intelligence, that you call your mental mind, to be able to think, feel, and see beyond the little dimension in which you are living. When you go to your place of study, we would ask you to think about and find the answer for the words; kingdom, dimension, light, and darkness. When you have these enlightened visions with you, while you are thinking, you will be able to get on the outside of your mental intelligence where you find the wisdom and the use of your God-mind. We have no condemnation for the way any religious movement is taught. We have no condemnation for any practice that will help any student to be able to still this physical self to receive these great vibrations of their higher realm. We do say never to allow anyone to impose their mental power upon you or anyone that may interfere with you in receiving.* For once anybody has imposed their mental

*Hypnotism

23

power upon you, you are never free from it in that life and sometimes many lives are spent in seeking that freedom. When you have something about which you want to know or understand, write it down or converse with someone and, in time, it will be revealed to you.

To say that you have lived even as far as the beginning of the Adam creation is so and you might not understand why but I do hope you will understand before your time on earth is finished. This pattern that you have each been given; your light pattern, is the book of which you hear so many teach. It is written in the book; for your records show where you have failed and where you have gained and your guardian angel is the one that will reveal to you where your weakness is and where your strengths have been. When you take up another body and return to earth, you have all those weaknesses that you must overcome.

Pray tell me why you cannot understand that those who have misery, who have heartaches, who have loss and poverty; why they have them? Not because God is punishing them but because that is the pattern they took to overcome hatred, malice, anger, lust and passion; all of the sinful things of life you call temptations. When they have erased any one of the seven deadly sins, their pattern becomes less and less, until they are the overcomer. Then and then only do you overcome death because, when you have overcome, you do not have to go into spirit-land. You ascend into the Master Kingdom where you take up the work of the salvation of all people upon the earth. When those on earth find that they have more trouble, more heartache than they seem to be able to bear, that is when God loves them the most because he sees them big enough, strong enough, wise enough to be the overcomer. No one is permitted that which is beyond his ability. So, my Children, as you go on the path of light, remember the only way you know you have strength is to be tested. If you can be tested without error, you can be the overcomer. If you have weaknesses, it is better to find them. Strength is not a glory except that you can help someone else. That is the education that is going on in spirit-land, the same as it is going on earth, for many masters are teaching in spirit-land about how to overcome death, the same as we are endeavoring to teach you on earth.

To speak to you of your past lives would not bring to you much glory nor would it give you enlightenment of what your future is to be. My endeavor in coming each day is to help you be prepared that you may enter into the Temple which is in the mountain. We have heard and many have been seeking the temple in the forest, with the seven spires and the roof of gold which reflects into the sky that many say they have seen. But there is no temple with a gold roof with seven spires. I say that there are twelve councilors in the Temple. I am the elder brother of the council. We often have with us the thirteen Councilor but he goes all over this earth to many places He is accepted here as the greatest teacher the earth has ever known. I leave with you peace, that you may be able to think calmly, to reason, and find a great understanding. I bless you with harmony that you may vibrate with your soul and, when the soul is in tune with your physical mental mind, great things can be revealed. For the eye that sees on earth does not see as the eye of the soul. I bless thee with the abundance of love to fill all needs and to help you to be generous with all about you. Amen, Amen, Amen.

CHAPTER IV

THE RACES UPON EARTH

Beloved Children, I too have heard your prayers; I too join in your prayer that God has blessed you and we are thankful for it; that your days shall be filled with great wisdom; that you will store what we teach you in your storehouse and take it out and use it when you can understand it. I read your thoughts when you were thinking about the time the people followed Jesus, your Teacher, upon the sands to hear him talk to teach the truth and, like them, you have come high on the mountain where the ways of the world are forgotten that you may be taught by teachers of truth. I heard your prayers when you said that God had given his angels charge over thee and today I shall tell you how God looks after His children, that they may find the path that leads them upward and not the path that holds them bound to earth. In the kingdom which includes the fourth and fifth dimensional activities around the earth, you will find the kingdom of the Angels and the Masters. And God so loved His children that He gave His only begotten Son that He may bear light to the children of the earth that they may find and know the God in them and that they too are the Sons of God. When God saw upon the earth the great mixing of lives with no light to guide them, no dependable words that they might hear to encourage them to believe in truth, God gave them His angels which includes angels that guard life, the angels that inspire, the angels that give them prayers, the angels that give them knowledge, and those that guide the life and death pattern of all living beings on earth. That they should be guided in the right direction as to their educational program of wisdom, God has sent His messengers; those that you shall know and term the masters, the ascended masters.

Those angelic beings that God had sent to earth and who became enmeshed in earth's temptations and who have ascended back over death; those who now understand the problems of the earth-life, they are given charge over the ascending races. Before I shall give to you the works of the masters, I shall tell you a little about the races upon the earth, so that you may know to what race you belong and why you have not understood it before. Every word I shall give of direction of understanding is found in your bible. You may have a hand with this information now to work with and I shall repeat that the word god is not a singular word and that there are many gods of creation.

There are twelve gods that rule the living beings upon your earth. Each god's creation results in different types of beings. If you will go back through your earth as a development, as a planet millions of years ago and when it first became inhabited, the people created then were not like you, and you are not like them. They were built that they could stand the ruggedness of their planet. They were built with understanding enough to take care of themselves as a race of people. They lived in animal instinct and not human instinct. Each period or age or change of your earth brought forth another race of people and they were also human beings upon your earth. Later, another race was developed by another god. These races had no heavenly aspirations. It was true they died of flesh and were born again from the lowest realm of spirit-land and, in thousands and thousands of years, there was very little change. There was no soul contact with them whatsoever. Great groups that were born on earth were under the direction of an oversoul, like the plant, mineral and animal kingdoms, though their oversoul was not of the same type. The last division is the root race of all people.

This last race that I speak of is the last root race that was created upon the earth. This last race was the Yehovah God race, giving you four root races upon your earth up until this time. Now, these races, to get your mental mind thinking, were found many places all over the earth. From each one of these root races, many mixed races and tribes of human beings have developed. They were known as the black, brown, yellow, and white root races. But as yet, only the white had the soul contact; all others were oversoul living beings. The last race created has an individual mental mind and so began the upward turn of evolution for man. He began to see, think, and hear for himself by his physical desires, separating his thinking quality into action. Now, if you could possibly think back more than a few hundred thousand years, you will see the beginning of the races upon your earth.

The sub-races that come by evolution are the division that men make in their root races and these are called tribes. In your root races by marriage, as you call marriage, you bring forth a child that has the disposition from both parents and so on down does the tree of life exist in any root race and sub-race. The white root race that did not intermingle or mix with the bloods of any other root race kept a pure stream of the white root race, as every type of blood in any root race has its individual pattern. From that white root race has developed that white race you know today. As your bible tells you, there was a great flood. Let us not put a time limit upon it because none that have so far measured these periods of time have found an accurate measurement. It is enough to say that eventually, out of the white root race, came a man and his family that had kept that pattern pure, unadulterated, and that all others upon the earth of the white race had become intermingled with other root races, meaning they had become very wicked and the god that you have over the white race, as it is said in your bible, became angry and caused a great flood to destroy those on earth. Now, I would not contradict anyone who chooses to believe that the flood was all over the earth and destroyed all except those in a small boat, but I would rather include in these words that, where the white root race was gathered, there was a great flood and many, many thousands of people were drowned. If the water was all over the earth, which I cannot teach you, there must have been some little crevice or some tree that was higher or some mountain peak that was sticking out, for there were living people upon the earth after the flood. However, the importance of this message is that, after the great flood, there was only Noah and his family left of the light root race and, from that little mite of that pure light race there developed your divisions of the Israel race to which you belong.

If you will read your bible, you will find that there were twelve tribes of the light root race that were left. Noah was the sub-race of the white people or the white beings on the earth which now were mortal human beings, because they were the first race upon the earth to be able to have contact with the God mind. They were the first race to have individual contact with the God mind, knowing that there was an opportunity to overcome death and that the earth they lived upon as solid matter was the crudest state of their existence and that God had prepared for them a place in His mansions in the sky or in the heavens; the space for His children's real home. Because they would not have the understanding to refine this physical body and its thinking ability, they would not be able to live in that space home until they could return in a perfected state of existence. So began the process, by passing through the twelve tribes or the twelve divisions. In this way did man begin his cultivation for living life. It has taken many thousands of years; none can contradict. For those who can never feel that they have ever been on earth before, there are many reasons; one of which is that they have never wanted to know their higher self. They have not wanted to know the higher part of life; they have hung close to the earth.

Now, I would not leave you with the thought that God has forgotten all other root races upon the earth, for they, too, have their cultivation; their educational programs which are also evolving them into the higher state so that all races shall be lifted into the heavens. They are a part of the universe and the universe cannot exist without them. I say, think it over and, if you think that God is unjust because He has permitted four root races to grow and develop upon this earth, then I would say to you, "Oh, star, mighty star upon the heavens, why are you not the moon? Oh, moon, who sends thy tender light to earth, why are you not the sun?" And the answer shall come back, "In God's universe, everything has its place. Without it in its fulfillment, there would be no universe that would hold this earth planet; there would be no human beings upon the earth planet; there would be no space in the heavens that they could find as their matches."

Now, God has so provided that only the pure blood, the pure pattern out of each root race, could evolve unto its heavens. It is quite possible to trace back any one of the root races. However, we are interested, at this time, in your light race. The unforgivable sin is the mixing of the race patterns. Even this is traced in your animals, in their life existence, where evolution stops. I do not mean to give you the impression that if two opposite race types should intermingle and bring forth an issue that God would not see and understand that pattern that came on earth. Although they would have nothing that would avail them of any great use as to their race development, their mentality can grow; their mind can grow and, when they do pass over into spirit-land division of which they would go, they are taught how to choose one or the other root pattern to which they belong. Do you not see that for every seed that is born on earth, it may take on any pattern it desires to learn and can come into whatever contacts on earth that will provide the channel? Yes, many students question, "Do I become of the black race when I go over on the other side, if I have, in any way, degraded or condemned the black race?" I say, it is possible that, if man, regardless of his race, will not learn; will not respect all other types of race, then he may have that opportunity and, when he has learned that lesson well and goes into what you term the fields where the harvests are plenty, into spirit-land, there he will be given the opportunity to take up which ever root race he has not learned and there he abides until he has become purified and, again when he goes to spirit-land, he may eventually evolve to his white race to which he belongs. This would apply to any other root race. They may take on a white body, that they may learn a lesson well, and go back into their root race from whence they came, that they may help the evolution of their root race.

Now, I speak to you of where you belong in this great evolution of the white root race. It would take many, many days of your time to form the context of the evolution of the white root race. The most important part with which I can impress you today is that, as the white race spreads, the twelve tribes spread over your earth continents. You have seen continents go down and rise; you have mingled and intermingled with other races, but chosen from light races upon the earth are the pure tribes. America was chosen as the bed of the Israel. The question arises, "How come there are so many other races in America besides the Israel?" All of those root races that are here are the ones that their races are depending upon to learn the evolution, the completion, of their root races.

Do I give you the impression that there are millions of white tribes that belong to your root race and only those in America are the Israel? To some extent, that is true, but that does not mean that God will forget all other people upon the earth, for He has given His angels charge over them. The Israel are the refined mind and bodies that form the part of the Sons of God who had taken on flesh bodies in every root race to help their lesser fellowman and failed. But, because they are part of the universal plan of this earth, they are passing through experiences that make them a vital part in fulfilling God's plan for the earth. We did not say planet; we said the earth. Out of every one of the periods of change on the earth, so many out of each root race are capable of elevating to the place in the planet space or universal space around this earth to where they belong and where they come again upon the earth.

There is no ceasing of evolution, either upon the earth or in man. There is no way to escape whatever part in which you belong and you may delay the time over and over again. Now, I would call to your attention once again to say to you that the flood that is spoken of in your bible was not the only destruction upon the earth. It has passed through many dangers. God was not destroying life. No God that ever created life would destroy it. This life that met death was trained and taught again in spiritland and sent back to earth. Each time it returned a little higher, both in mental mind and, eventually, the God mind, growing toward evolution and its place in God's Kingdom.

I would call your attention to your bible again and say that, if you read it by word, comparing it to what you believe is the meaning of the word of today, you fail to find the deep understanding. There was no individual person as Adam and no individual person as Eve. Adam represented the pure man of the Israel race and Eve represented that pure channel of the Israel race. Adam represents the God-mind and Eve represents the mental brain mind. Through the processing of male and female has come the refined part of all twelve tribes. As the word Adam means living light, it also represents perfection. As Eve represents the mother, the process that all must pass through to live on earth, she represents a pure substance formation, never having been adulterated by mixture of any other type or race or even sub-race or root race. Therefore, at the time that Adam and Eve were created, it was not because they were the first man-body or woman-body, but because that was the beginning of the twelve tribes of the pure Israel race. Then, and then only, was it pure enough to be called the Sons of God.

Dear Children of Earth, I do not desire to disturb your world of thinking nor would I destroy your belief in God. If it helps you, I will say that, if you will take each part I give to you and review it, thinking and pondering over what has been called the mysteries of God's creation, you will see how it will unfold to you the reason why for every-

31

thing. Do not accept it as a whole cloth until you have committed yourself by your own thinking. There you will find the great joy within yourself of knowing who you are, why you are, and from what space you came and to where you shall return. This is evolution of man.

No place in your bible will you ever find that God loved the white root race better than He loved the black root race, nor the yellow, nor the brown. Eventually, there will be nothing left behind. It may be that some of the black root race have evolved so fast that they may be there to greet you when you appear as an advanced soul. I advise you to return back and read your bible and study the words that man has so placed as stumbling stones in his light of learning.

I read before me the mind of one who is asking, "Are our angels white?" I can give you the answer. How you will know it is truth, I cannot say, but when you understand the meaning of beings that are of the angel kingdom, you will understand that there is no male nor female; no black or white. Their likeness is not as a mortal being but, as a human spiritual being would be created, only of mind. Their illumination is so crystal white that you could not say it is blue, black, yellow, or brown.

I suggest that you have a rest period every day, whether you lie down or sit in the shade of a tree somewhere, and where you can be individually thinking your own thoughts; resting without the sound of words. Amen, Amen, Amen.

CHAPTER V

WHAT ARE YOUR BODIES

Awaken Children, from dreamland. I will tell you of realities that you cannot see, cannot find, cannot hold. They are not dreams; they are reality. It was the first time I had seen Phylos walk from us towards the tree and the first time I had seen his back. His back was like a cross. I thought that this was what Jesus had meant when He took up His cross. It was not a wooden cross, but of flesh, as we bear it with us all the time we are in the physical body yet we do not see it, but feel its effect.

I give you the greeting of the Great White Brotherhood. My soul greets thee, Children of Earth. My heart is filled with love for all fellowman. I shall give you words of truth. I give praise to God on high. Amen, amen, amen.

I shall speak to you about your existence upon earth and how you make the changes through death so that you will recognize where there is neither male nor female in the ascended ones. While you work upon the earth in your last life pattern, your physical body is male and female. Your invisible body is female insofar as positive and negative energies are concerned. The misconception of the words male and female are only name tags upon your physical bodies on earth. Because the male body originally was the strongest, physically and mentally, they called him male. Because the female, which means mother, was the one who attracts to the earth the incoming seeds, they called it female or mother. Therefore, in your earth bodies, you recognize the difference of form. There is coming a day soon that the male will not be the strongest, but he will still be the positive male man. Science has not given the clear meaning of what was meant by positive and negative. In your flesh body, they mean the positive body which means flesh and you call **alive.** In the body you do not see as it is invisible, is a substance body which is the female or negative body. Science, of itself, understands, but man, who reads their language, does not have a clear version of it. You see, in the use of your bodies, the one that is visible is positive and the one that is invisible is negative. It means that which is visible is made of substance matter but ruled by mind energies and that which is invisible and negative is ruled by soul energy. This is the reason that, in our way of seeing life, we say you are in the death body. When you are in spirit-land, you are in the life body. The life body is pure substance. In your earth body, it is a constant change of life and dying, for man is under the law of the seven steps of death and the seven deadly sins.

So that you will understand the words that I shall use when I speak of four of your body actions, that you may be clear on which one I am speaking, I here give you the names. Your soul body, that you recognize as your higher

self, is the Christness of you; your God mind. Your next body is that which is called your spirit body, spirit meaning life, and it is your pattern body, your life body, which, in the beginning you created and will continue to create until you have returned. It is referred to as the 'breath of life,' but because it does not have two arms, two legs and teeth, as you have in this physical body, it does not change the truth that it is a body. Then you have your life and death bodies; the bodies that you pass into; one into the other. That which you call your ghost body, or shadow body, is a substance physical body. It has two arms, two legs and everything that you have on earth except it has no weight, it does not digest food and it does not have a circulatory system for its blood does not circulate. It has only your nervous system and mental physical brain; the lower mind that is referred to in many writings.

When you are born as a babe and come into flesh existence, the unfolding of your pattern begins with your first breath. Immediately upon hearing this, some say, "Why are our past lives hidden if we live over and over again?" I would say, man would be in a terrible state if he did not have the door closed behind him until he has come to the place on the path of life that he can recognize and adjust life accordingly. The veil is between the visible and the invisible worlds. Therefore, when a babe is born according to its surrounding atmosphere; its physical contact; and its intellectual development; according to all of this is the unfolding in the use of its mentality.

So, when I speak of your soul, I speak of the God mind in you. When I speak of your spirit, I am speaking of your breath of life; your pattern. When I speak of your shadow body, I am speaking of the body you enter into when you pass through the change of death. When I speak of your life body, I am speaking of your physical body that you demonstrate by walking, talking, and living upon your physical earth as a human being.

Now, as to when man came on earth and how he came on earth is, indeed, a long story. It would be too much for you to endeavor or attempt to consume as knowledge. Only as you climb the paths towards your higher self, can it be unfolded in security for students on

34

the path of life. There is a past and a future. Neither one can be of benefit to you except right now. For those who would like to know who they were in past lives, once they have accepted the idea of rebirth and death, incarnation and re-incarnation; if they would like to know who they were as to persons on earth, I speak to each student on the path of light and say that it does not matter who you were in your past lives; whether you were a king or queen or early laboring slave. What you accomplished in the past is all that affects you now. All that was in your past is of no avail to you unless you have something inherited by which to live. All that matters to man on earth is what he is doing with his life today. Your future you cannot live unless you take on new life and there you will unfold what you have lived today. I would not advise you to say you have not had a past or that the future does not matter, for all you have accomplished in the past is what you are today and all that is in your future is how you use your time and energy today.

Now, I advise all students who start on the unfold-ment of spiritual light and wisdom to be sure and under-stand every problem they attempt to unfold, for without understanding a wise man is lost. I would also advise all students who seek the light to make their steps after they have cemented their will to the higher mind, the one of unselfishness. In other words, to become selfless. How do I mean this? I will say to you that, as a sheath of grain has a number of seeds, you cannot go through your fields and pluck one seed; you must harvest all seeds. So it is with man on earth today. Each is responsible for those that surround him. So you cannot be saved unless you make efforts to save others. You are not selfless so long as you seek only for yourself. When Yessue Ben Miriam, who lived on earth as Jesus the Christ, taught His bless-ings of truth, He did not say salvation for one or a few; he said salvation for all. So, whenever you attempt to find good for yourself, do good for someone else. Whenever you feel you have earned a spiritual understanding, be sure to share it with someone else. Whenever you feel that you have been blessed with the earth's supplies you call wealth, you will never know the joy of it or that God has blessed you with abundance or the joy that comes with it until you share it with someone else. Whenever

you have felt the blessings of peace and harmony in your surroundings, how can you know its value unless you share it with someone else?

If you have health and are active in life, do not set those aside that you call aged because they are not as active as you or because you do not think that they are up to your standard of thinking. Only when man has started on the down steps of life by age is he capable of understanding the value of life. If you have the health, do for those who have not the health. Share with them the ability of movement by doing for them the things they cannot do for themselves. The sadness upon awakening in the change called death is when you have to face the patterns that you have forgotten to be kind to older attendants in life. When you think of these words, you will see that the foundation of your culture upon earth is formed from respect, and honor, and truth, and kindness, in selflessness.

Now, I would like to advise you on my part of the service. I have told you that we are the ascended ones. To begin at the beginning, or take up from today, would leave you in doubt of many things that are essential for you to know. How can the heavenly host visit upon your earth and assist you? All of this knowledge cannot be learned or even become practical to believe unless you have the whole truth; past, present, and future. As to the beginning of a record, I am forming words for you to be able to pass through these coming months until you come here again to learn the beginning of life's story from its very conception concerning you.

Inside the mountain is a gathering of the hosts of those who descend down to earth to help their fellowman to overcome death. They work from this place because it is essential that their presence must be changed from one dimension to a lower dimension to work and be recognized. Therefore, the shadow body, of which you call your physical body, takes on a certain amount of density, but it is not a flesh matter body and that is the type of body we use. It is called truly a physical body but it is not a matter/germ body. I hope you will think this over to find a definite conclusion of truth. This body is capable of appearing as a dense body or it can disappear from your vision by changing its element state but it does not die.

You have seen me go through the motions of what you call walking, yet, I do not have to walk. There is no need for me to walk, for there is no distance but the ever-present now. Because you cannot go through the form of being here, and your thought awakening elsewhere, does not mean that it cannot be done. I can watch you as you are sleeping and see you attending to a chore at a later time. This would be what you are intending to do in the future as actual work, yet you would not recognize it as such. The body in which you are living must go through certain motions to cover the distance that is between here and there. If I were to tell you that you do not have to burn wood for heat, you would not understand that I mean on this side of life you do not have to start a fire as you do by adding a flame created from something else and on down. Your very thought, if you know how to use your thought, would be able to produce the ever-burning flame; the fire that takes out all impurities in the air and leaves only purity in its place. When I tell you that you need not go through the process of growing a tree to produce fruit after many years; that you can immediately reach out in the atmosphere and have that fruit; all of this would sound impossible to you but it is the truth. Only explanations and the actual attempt of use will bring to you the reality of this certain type of manifestation.

In this particular place, high up on the mountainside, there are a host of us. I am not alone. We work from this advantageous point to reach man by the thought activity of energy. We are in contact with thousands and thousands on this side of the mountain and what you term your West Coast. We have charge over most of the eight western states in this United States. Over this whole world of yours there have been many points from which the heavenly hosts work; guiding and directing the nations and the people as tribes and guiding and directing this spiritual growth of individuals. At the present time, there are seventeen such places upon your earth. How long all of them will be active depends upon your future and its control of the world as nations. In this particular place on this mountain, you may call it an Inner Temple, for Temple means a place of God's work and worship, and worship means work. There are twelve who are constantly working with a certain amount of human beings called mortal human beings, thinking human beings, that belong to a certain classification for ascension.

When I speak thus, I am not speaking selfishly as of a choice. I would not deny truth to any human being seeking it. I give freely and I endow each one to also give freely to others. In this Temple, not many human feet have entered, but many who have been on the path of light have been taken there in their invisible body by their higher self and those who have been put in charge of them. Some remember and some are afraid and will not speak about it. We can show the way of light that is best to follow, but we do not dictate, we do not command, nor do we ever demand of anyone. Whatever path they choose to follow, that is the path on which we will help them. Until they of themselves change, we do not make changes for them.

I am sure my elder brother, a councilor in the Inner Temple, shall come and guide you on a walking journey soon. Another elder brother shall come and converse with you when I will not be here. If all goes well and you follow instructions, we shall lead you up on the mountain before you return to your home. There will be certain rules and regulations to help you in your preparation of going up on the mountain and we would like to have you follow them for your own good, for a helping hand to your own physical ability. These instructions I will give to you on our next visit here. If it is possible for you to keep in mind any questions that you would like to be revealed to you for a cleared vision of understanding, I will serve you well.

My blessings, my Children of Earth. May the rest of your day be one of joy. May you find in the service that the masters extend to you a peace you have not known before. May, in the future, your worldly trials be met with stronger intentions of good than you have had in the past because of fears and doubts. When the world, and we speak of the world as the people who form the existence upon the earth, is in its great distress, remember that purification is taking place, both in your race and all races upon the earth. When you send out your thoughts of blessings, peace, harmony and love, send them to all corners of the earth, which means everywhere. For, as you send them off, God will see that they reach where they are most needed. Amen, Amen, Amen.

CHAPTER VI

EVOLUTION AND THE UNIVERSE

Children of Earth, I give to you the greeting of the Great White Brotherhood. My soul greets thee. I, Phylos stand in what you have called illumination but what you actually vision is your fourth dimension. There is no darkness in the fourth dimension. Because you live in the third dimension activities where all things are solid, that which is manifested is in the solid and that which is to be manufactured is the substance formula of it in the night side of life, as you call it, it is invisible until it manifests. That explains for you that, when many see visions, they speak of the light that is around them. You can tell from what part of the dimensions they come from by the light. This light that you see here is everywhere in the fourth dimension. You are only visioning the amount of what your eye can take in of the fourth dimension because I have the power, or ability, to manifest a physical form in the light to you. Whenever you see a master, an angel, or one from the heavenly realm, they will have this light around them. Later I will tell you how you can compare it to what you have around you. If you should see another being appear to you, often, in what appears to be a spirit form, even the manifestation of the appearance of the physical body, you may see a bluish-white light around them as a vapor but it has no gleam to it and it does not come from the fourth dimension. That is still in your third dimension and there is good and evil that can perform in those conditions. On your physical plane, you call this the aura around both the departed spirits from earth and your physical forms. Though you do not always see the auras around those in a physical form, it is possible to be seen. In this aura, you liken it to the planet earth being in its uniform, or in the universe that surrounds the earth. This uniform is divided into patterns, or layers, of ether. Around each physical body, it is divided into three layers of energy forces. It is your universe and you are the earth. As above, so below. All plans for greater, all plans for the lesser; this is existence in the universe that contains your earth.

While I speak of the universe, I will give you one more thing that you may put on your records that you shall study. Every planet with which you are acquainted as to your astronomy has its own universe, the same as this earth has its universe. You could not enter on or into the universe that surrounds the planet unless you pass through the type of layers of its aura, the same as you must penetrate to get to this earth through its type of aura to get out. All other parts of the universe of the great universe, that contains each planet universe, is the darkness and the deep of which your bible speaks as 'in the beginning.'

I also state here for your consideration that you have known planets that science has accepted, but there are many planets of which you do not yet know but will, in the coming years, keep adding until you have many more than what you have now. As far as the stars are concerned in the heavens that you see, you only can find the information by certain placements of stars in your heavens and those stars rule your universe. All science refers to the center of your universe as your sun, when actually the sun is not in the center of your universe; not your earth's universe. It is on the oustide of your universe, the same as all the stars are on the outside of your universe. All the planets that you see pass through your universe but are not always in it. Therefore, the times that they pass through your universe, you feel their intense rays and, when they are on the outside of your universe in space and perhaps in other universes, you do not feel their intense ray but you feel the effect of their intense rays as they are still in your universe. Their rays affect the elements upon your earth. The sun affects all life energy upon earth and, when they are in conjunction with the sun's rays, you have great progress upon your earth. When they are not in conjunction with the sun's rays, you have a slower retarding action upon your earth, as well as in the human beings.

I do not wish to upset your thinking of what science

has placed in your thinking that you have something on which to go, but I will give to you a few thoughts as to how you, as man, cannot always have solved the problems, even though it might be reasonable. There are still some problems that have not been solved and I speak of it that you may cause your mental thinking to reach out, for as long as you keep your mental thinking focused upon what you can absorb, you do not get away from your earthly thinking and, therefore, your mental mind is not capable of understanding that which is outside of your realm. So, what I give to you is to help your mentality as to stretching it so as to be able to absorb farther out away from the earth. These words may help you fill in some of your idle moments.

Have you ever thought, as long as you can remember, that the earth revolves on its axis and that when you are up you may be upside down? Have you ever thought that you never see the stars except at night when you are away from the sun? Then the stars cannot be where the sun is located. The stars must be out in space away from, or on the outside of, your universe and, when you see the stars, you are actually seeing the outside to the beginning of your universe limitations. That space may have great distance, as you know distance on earth, as they reckon by measurement of stars by daylight or light years. Yet your eyes, built only for the third dimension, can actually see beyond many dimensions. Each layer around the earth is likened to a dimension and you have seven layers, that we call belts, around your earth.

Now, do not believe that you may have to take what I have said in words, as your law or authority. We give you this portion so that in your times where you are able to place yourself in quiet thinking, you can perhaps talk about them.

I want to refer to your bible, as you have brought it with you. I desire you to open to the first chapter in your bible. In that first chapter, the history that is given there of the beginning of the creation is what I want to show you as to how man reads by words that his intelligence, or memory, may be broadened and filled with trust and faith in something he does not understand. I am sure you have heard many teachers say, "The letter of your bible killeth, but the spirit of the bible giveth eternal life." I am sure you have heard many who teach claim they have read the bible so many times, from cover to cover. Perhaps they do not tell you they have learned to read by spirit, not by letter, and yet they do not teach it by spirit; they teach it by letter. Most earth students and teachers believe that God created man as you see him in a flesh body and that His first creation of man made a fall in sin and now all the children that are born since that time suffer death and pain, and still now find salvation. I want to point out to you that in that first chapter it speaks of the light above and it speaks of waters, seas, and oceans. It speaks of the dividing of what is above and what is below. If you think it means the seas, the great bodies of water that you have around your continents, you are mistaken. It does not. It is speaking of the spaces around your earth; the belts of which I have just spoken. When it speaks of the light, do you think it speaks of the sun that you see in daytime? Do you think that, when it speaks of the 'other light,' it speaks of the moon? It does not. The greater light is that which is the God mind and the lesser light is your mental thinking mind.

Now, many preach from their pulpits that God created Adam, but nowhere in your bible will you find that God created Adam. In your first chapter in the last eight verses it tells that Gods created the formula of man; that Gods created man and looked upon him and found the image good. This took place on the sixth day. Now, it does not say Monday, Tuesday, Wednesday, etc. It does not say that, so there is something left unexplained. Gods created the image of Gods and called it man, male and female. But do you know what 'man' means? Do you know what 'image' means? There is your answer to God's creation; not God but Gods' creation.

In reading your story of Adam and Eve, you will find in all history, all records that are authentic of this earth, that for many millions of years there have been beings called human beings upon this earth. There have been attempts to believe and teach that the evolution of man began with the small creeping things from the water. But I say to you, "No." The man, the image, the formula that Gods created never began with anything that was not like the image of Gods and, I am sure, the Gods are not the image of any animal of earth.

So, this first creation of the Gods was a formula of perfect man; a perfect race. He called them the Sons of God. Now it was decided, and I use the word decided, meaning the decision of the Gods, that these Sons of Gods should have the opportunity to have an individual mind of God. All other beings on the earth did not have the individual God mind; they had the mental thinking mind. They had no individual soul but they had the oversoul, so all responsibility of their progression came under the Gods that created them and their ambassadors who were in charge of them. It had nothing to do with this creation that the Gods created, for They had created a formula that would be able to perceive and conceive Godliness. So the greater light was created, the God mind, to shine upon this creation that is the Sons of God and illuminate their mental mind and join it together; the greater light and the lesser light. The Gods gave to their workers, the Lord Gods, the power to give them movement of individuality.

It was Lord God that breathed and put this formula into action and created a soul body to contain the God mind, so that each formula that was created into an individuality would have their own portion equally placed at their use. Then it was decided that they would descend these beings created to the earth to work among the races of people that were on earth; the black, brown, and yellow races that were on earth that did not have individual minds of God but were under the universal soul mind called oversoul to guide them. Now, where this creation takes place of the soul existence is the Melchizedek Order which I desire you to call in your thinking, the Master Kingdom. It was a kingdom all its own. Each kingdom has work to do concerning the earth; the beings on earth, not the earth itself.

After this soul existence of man had developed into individuality and could be, as it were, taught law and order, then they had to have a body with which to work. So the conception between the God that you call the Yehovah and the other Gods was that they would create a condition that would cause life and death. They would create two forms that could stay on earth until the solution of all the problems of man could be solved.

For this reason the medium of existence to stay on earth was created; to have spirit-land and the earth so as to know its solidness. The eve body which was next created of man was the body that you now call your physical body. When it is born into your earth existence, it can be controlled by gravity and cannot lose its way from earth except by death and it is called a solid body; physical flesh matter. Time limitation was placed upon that man to live so long upon the earth and, when he could not learn anymore and could not manifest any further his mental thinking in contact with the God mind, he passed into what is called death; into the substance invisible body. Then by his higher self, his own soul individual God mind is taught how again to eliminate that which would dissolve his ability and hold him to earth and give him an opportunity to come back in his flesh body again and learn, step by step, his own individual Godliness called the Sons of God. I would like to add here that this is the beginning of your light race.

Now, those of you who say that there are many races of people all over this world, and what about them? Did not God, in the beginning, create this earth, your planet? Did not the Gods create all beings upon the earth? But let me add the most thinkable part of the solution and that is that if you have in any way interfered with the pattern of your blood, you may have parts of all races in your blood which makes it not pure. Only those who have never interfered with the pattern of their blood of the light race are the Sons of God. Always hold that in your conception of truth.

I am sure you are going to say, "All this is beyond my thinking ability. What has that to do with me? I will take my chance. I am as God created me and I will do the best I can." I say that sometimes the best is only a poor attempt and that, for those who are thinking of what life is, of what it was meant to be, to think deeply on the meaning of the races; of the meaning of the word 'God,' forgetting that when you say God, you mean Gods; that when you say light, you are not speaking of the sun that you know as daylight, but of the higher mind and the lesser light of the lower mind; that you cannot save your soul by your mental mind but you can join it to the God mind in you and come forth as a shining light in the fourth dimension, for all masters are in the fourth dimension.

44

All masters, who are as you see standing before you, have overcome death. Those that have not lived on earth, do not come to earth, but do appear in the sky so you may know that the angels have been placed over you.

I will recount to you what you have at your command. When you were sent to earth to become a soul incarnated into a flesh man, one of God's high sources were placed in charge of you. He has been with you from the time you have raised above your mental thinking capacity and have taken on the possibility of the God mind. Each time you have returned to earth in a flesh body, he has been with you to help you in every step of the path of light. He is not interested in your personality; he is interested only in your individuality. When you have made your first step of desiring to know more about the Gods, more about your spiritual understanding, every attempt to rise above your personality or your earth existence, you have added to your group of angels, helpers, and other masters, until you have ten masters to guide you, keep you, guard you, and protect you from being enmeshed into the underworld. With each step, called death, you rise above, until the time comes when you will overcome death and never die by death, yet you do die many times. With each of you, when you were born and God first gave Lord God permission to create your soul existence, your guardian angel was placed with you to keep your pattern pure; to bear all records of all your lives while you are in the generation from the Son of God to the lowly flesh man and back again to your Sonship of God. Amen, Amen. Amen.

CHAPTER VII

VIBRATIONS AROUND YOU

I give to you the greetings of the Great White Brotherhood. This is the order of the Melchizedek Kingdom. My soul greets thee. My heart is filled with love for all fellowman. I shall speak words of truth, giving praise to God on high. I am Phylos.

(At this time, Phylos' voice began softly and had a musical tone to it. This I cannot explain, but, if you have ever heard how the string of a violin will keep sounding long after the finger has been taken away, you will understand. That is the way his voice seemed to come to us; as though you could hear the sounding of the last words as he was talking on.)

Beloved Children of Earth, I come to you to give light and understanding. I will endeavor to take apart many of your word terms that give cause and effect.

I speak of the word 'light.' I do not refer to the effects of candle or oil or of your electricity or any other type of illumination that you have on your earth. This light of which I speak is from a higher dimension and affects your faculities that give you the possibility of seeing the cause of every effect and the effect that causes every cause. The illumination that you term a 'gleaming light' is had by every being that has overcome death and is risen to the third realm of the Melchizedek Order. This illumination ascends; coming out through the top center of your head. Only when your faculties which work with the seven nerve centers of your body have risen, in effect, above your physical body, can this illumination be produced. It is the light that surrounds your earth.

Now I would take you back to your day of silence and explain to you that what each of you refer to as trust, belief, and faith are actually things in action. If you will, remember to place in your everyday thinking mind that when we use the word 'thing,' we are referring to that which has been created and has its own pattern and, when we are speaking of 'stuff,' as to mind stuff, we are referring to that prana, essence, and mind of which all things that are on earth are created from. You cannot create one thing unless you have the material out of which to create it. This universe has much essence, much prana, and much mind stuff. All creation upon your earth that has life is made of prana, essence, and mind. If you get away from the idea that upon your earth you must cut, hew, or mold everything you have, you will find that all you can learn is in space around and about you in your very thinking, long before you are able to place your hands upon it.

I would like to give to you future work from the Temple

46

so that you can see that you do not live only for today, but that we live and act for tomorrow; for the future. Why do we have a place high on this mountain? Like all other living things in God's Kingdom, the higher you are in your altitude, the purer is the atmosphere. The atmosphere of which I speak is invisible to you because it belongs to another dimension. This is the altitude of the God mind in you. This God mind in each of you becomes useless to you when you are around other vibrations, confusions, and misinterpretations. Only those who are capable of aspiring to the higher methods of thought, called vibrations, are capable of living and existing mentally or spiritually or physically in the higher altitudes. The higher your altitude, the less world confusion. If you can imagine in your understanding of how things multiply, I will suggest to you that the thinking of many people is alike. If you take one drop of water and put it in a large bucket or container, it will not make much of an impression, will soon evaporate and go away and be forgotten. If many of you put one drop of water in a bucket, soon your bucket will be filled and it will not fade away and it will not evaporate; it will even multiply itself. That is the same with each of you when you are down in the world of confusion. You may think you are alone and, in your thinking about thoughts and forms and things, you may be inside a building where you say you are alone, yet thoughts can pass through anything you have on your earth as to walls and, soon, all thoughts are joined together that are of the same type and gradually, unknown to you who exist on earth, these balls of thought, and I will call them balls as they are gathered together as a cloud, float around in the space above many of you. There you gather as groups and, by your electric or your magnetic attraction, you attract certain clouds of thoughts. Some are despondent, some are destructive. Sometimes the clouds are constructive and that is the type that float around above the 3,000 foot level. Because many are gathered together in places, even though they do not know they are of a group, they feel the results. I hope you think on this until it becomes a reasonable possibility, although you do not see it now. This is the world of thought and the world of thinking. There must be the attraction before you can realize its effect. Here, where you are high on the mountain, you are above the clouds of thoughts of confusion, enmity, war, hatred, malice and wickedness in many forms.

Those of you on earth who have small children should know that until they are seven years of age, the type of thoughts that are attracted by the parents hover over those children and begin their future pattern. If the parents feel that they have not the responsibility, I would say to them, awaken. Awaken, for your future depends upon it. Be not afraid to admonish, to criticize those parents who will not see the future for their children.

How do we work from the Radiant Temple? To get into the higher altitude where there is not the impurity of thought, we get into the celestial vibration that you on earth call 'rays of vibration.' Your science has endeavored to classify them as colors and, if you will take apart your words on earth you call speed, time, and sound, you will find they are each divided into many vibrations and they must have a combination to reach your earth from the celestial realms around your earth. To every faculty and nerve center that each of your bodies have; that is, if the body is a normally formed body, there is a ray combination of light vibrations. They stimulate and develop your faculties so that you are able to see by understanding and they stimulate your nerve center so that your brain becomes a developed seat of the heavenly father. Would I tell you that they would only act upon you as to comfort and enfold you? I would be telling you what was not true, for everything that is created on your earth you can misuse and the result may even be death. So, I speak of these rays as being dangerous, yet they are the gift of God to man but, if you misuse the vibrations of the higher source, the celestial, you find evil results; evil because it is destructive. God so found that, in making the connection of the God mind in a solid form in man, connected with his mental mind, there had to be a safe source of carriage, and that source He has placed in the angels He gave charge over each one of you.

There are those on earth who are partaking of the vibrations of these rays, not knowing how they do it. Many find that they are destructive, for if these rays are too intense for the mental cells of your body, they will destroy them and there you will find the mentally dis-

48

turbed. We are speaking of those who have lost reason in madness. We are speaking of those that you say are mentally disturbed. Sometimes many are confined in what you term your institutions or hospitals, under medical care, but, if the cell is destroyed, there is no repair. God, in his wisdom, has chosen those who will apply of the Azrael, the ray directly under the care of their guardian angels, that they will never have such trouble. Only by the proper use of unfoldment can it be secure and dependable. Every angel that is put in charge of your contact of God mind into the mental mind must develop a sense faculty that will be connected, both visible and invisible, to the objects on earth; the reason of them and the possibilities of God substance is not visible.

On earth, you term it science; the developing of intellect, but God does not get the credit. Man's intelligence of mental mind receives the credit. God does not mind. God includes all; there is nothing left out. The law of security of God mind and mortal mind is when, as you develop your sense understanding called your knowledge or ability of intelligence, God develops, by use of the rays, each of your God mind faculties so that you can understand the cause and effect of past, present, and future. When they are equally divided, each using the same amount of power, the God mind in you is perfect and that is the term of understanding. When you pray for wisdom, never forget to pray and give thanks for understanding.

How does a person figure, in his understanding, why some are good and some are bad or evil? Those who are good are no better than those who are bad or evil, as far as God is concerned. Those who are good; those who are using the God mind, are a little advanced. That is all. Every God mind on earth includes the mental mind on earth and, in its constant revolution and evolution, will find the same pattern that brings all together as the drops of water.

How does color develop, as you on the earth understand? Each of you have an aura; that part of space which belongs to the keeping or the making of your physical and spiritual existence. Your thinking affects the possibility that others can see the colors that are used and how they are used in your aura by your own thinking, physically and spiritually. The more tense and the more dense your physical mind thinks upon things, the deeper, coarser colors or combinations of tones that you use on earth are produced. The higher and the purer, the unadulterated, known as your shades of color, are those which have no denseness to them. There are times every aura has the higher rates of vibration but many are not aware of them. Even though the angels are about them, they are not aware of them, for they have no contact with their God mind and their mental mind rules them according to their ability of thinking on thoughts.

Why do we insist upon quietness? It is quite simple. On your earth, where there is quietness; where there is no confusion, there is no misunderstanding. In what you term your spiritual silence, you are only producing the possibilities of finding a space where there are no mixed thinking; no mixed thoughts. You may term it higher evolution.

When I speak of the regions of your earth, I tell you they are spaces on your earth, in your earth, and above your earth. Those above your earth are called spirit-land. It is a region that extends out from your earth as far as your air extends. Now, I did not say as far as your atmosphere extends; I said as far as your air, your breathing mixture of air extends, and in that region, is confined according to the realms, or divisions of it. There are realms in the division of the region of spirit-land. The region is a limitation. The world means condition. The planes are the ability of using the limitation of your earth mental thinking mind, or the contact of how much of your God mind you can use and what you are using, when you passed out from your earth life into your spirit, as you call it. We refer to is as the shadow body, for it is a physical body but is not solid. You are able to use what you have used on earth, in that body, and that is the plane upon which you will be. Your ability to use what you have evolved of the earth God mind in you, as I told you according to the thought clouds that hover about your children, is the plane in which you will be and, if you compare the likeness, you will understand. When you are in your meditation period, you will find that your thoughts will be likened to the level of the thought world. This means your ability to rise above spirit-land. Thoughts are not confined in spirit-land. They are in a world of their own. They may

50

not reach out any further than your atmosphere but they are limited to your density of earth.

I read in the thoughts in the ether about you. Each of you have, at times, expressed about the evolution of the plant kingdom and the animal kingdom. I will say to you that, as your evolution of man in his kingdom is surely visible to all of you in understanding, likewise in each one of the kingdoms there is an evolution. Perhaps you do not understand it because you do not see the change it takes. In every kingdom that is created upon your earth, there is evolution. Now, I would not tell you that the creeping things on earth become the animals of the future, for every division has its own evolution to its kind; in the mineral, the plant, and the animal kingdoms. If that were not true in those kingdoms, then what is true in your kingdom could not be true, either. For those who believe that they, in a new incarnation, can choose what they so desire to return to the earth, as they call it evolution, is not true. For those who believe they can come back in an animal existence, that is not true. There are certain truths that are affected by that type of thinking, but man does not change in his evolution to take on an animal existence, for animals are not created the same as humans are created. Although their division of thinking and ability of thinking may be crude as animals, you will find animals never take on cruelty.

I admonish, I ask and request all students of thought to rise to the angel's atmosphere of evolution. Angel means heavenly; angel means without solid earth flesh contact.

Now, in tomorrow's talk, I am going to go over again the division of your heavens as to creation and what exists in it. During the many months you will be away, you will have something to think about; to fathom and bring back in your coming year, for I request of you to come and be welcome here every year. You may come alone or you may come with many others. When I speak of aloneness, I mean those of you who are here now, or you may bring others with you. We welcome all who would desire to come and abide by your camp rules and abide by our way of living. Those who come may neither drink of the wines that dull your mental thinking nor may they smoke while they are on the holy ground of this mountain. Those who disobey, the masters will exclude.

If you come, I cannot say one or all will enter the Temple. There is one day each year, not always the same day or the same date of the year, that you may enter the Temple. We will advise you beforehand when that day comes and then you will have your day of silence and you will be of the understanding that you will be welcome the next day in the Temple. There you will be made acquainted with all the councilors that we were not capable of being permitted to give to you yesterday.

Remain in your seated position for five minutes after I am gone, for I shall not walk away. I will show you how I change from one body to the other.

I do not know how many more lessons you will be able to take with you, but we will give as many as possible. In your coming year, we will divide the lessons, beginning with the training of the physical man's mind so as to be able to transfer into the God mind in proper usage. I bless each one of you with love that is divine; with fellowship that is royal; with the highest of each of you as Beings of God meeting as the Children of God. Amen, Amen, Amen.

CHAPTER VIII

STAY ON YOUR OWN PATH

You can keep your numbers of months and years separated, as we do not have any past or future. All is in the now with which we work here. I am Emile (pronounced A-mile). I come to give to you a version of earth teachings in your spiritual terms, that you may know there are many paths upon which to travel that will teach the same core of truth. Your particular position, your circumstances, or your location have much to do with the path. I give to you the greetings of the Great White Brotherhood. My soul greets thee. My heart is filled with the love for all human existence. I shall give you words of truth, giving praise to God on high.

There are many different beings of truth that are in contact with people who have lived on your earth and have ascended. I am using the name of Emile who was my last protege, or student, on earth not too long ago. His work will continue until his life leaves his physical body and I shall wait his return upon earth again. I am one of the councilors at the Temple here. I have spent most of my priesthood in India, for, when I came to earth as a Son of God born in flesh, I was born among the brown people of the earth.

I shall correct any misconception of what are termed the brown and yellow races. The true forms of India are the evolved brown race. Many of them are still undeveloped. They are not the yellow race. They never have been. Like many other of your races, or tribes of races, there is some intermingling of blood pattern. I here speak only for the true brown race and I bring you close to that part of India, the Himalayan Mountains, where much of the training, of what is called the higher priesthood of man, takes place.

In the land of India of the true blood race, they have always had high and low class distinction, the same as you in your white race have high and low class; rich, poor; good, bad. You will notice that, in India, those who have not had any contamination with any other pattern, or tribe of other races, are the high class; they are the unadulterated. Those who have mixed blood patterns are the low class. They must serve in servitude to earn their freedom. They are barred from heaven and this classification has gone on for thousands of years.

It has always been a common knowledge that the first son born of any family was dedicated to priesthood. (In your English version, much that goes on in India among the elect, in your English expression, is not true. I am holding to the ancient version, though, if it should conflict with anything you have read or with what you come in contact as to your English version, I cannot be responsible for its truth. What I shall give to you now is as I have known it for thousands of years.) The selected ones are trained in their mental way of thinking but under the guidance of the spiritual training, or God mind, over matter. The children are taken at a very early age; when they can be weaned away from the parent, and they are put away from the world that they may not learn of wickedness. If, while you are living with the good and you do not hear or see any of the outside world expressions, you cannot miss it, for you do not know anything about it and, when you are secluded away from the mixtures of the world, it is very easy for you to follow a spiritual pattern. That is why they take the children quite early in their age; before they have made their seventh year to have begun to use their own thinking power.

While you, in your way of developing the body, think more of the abilities that the body can do and the perfect shape into which it can be put, and call it health. In seclusion they think less and less of their physical bodies and teach that above them is the heaven of which you on earth speak of as space. They believe it is their crown of glory and that, by despising and overcoming and mastering this physical body, they bring about the spirit taking over the body while you live. They teach you first to control the physical body and its movements. They do this by posture and thinking. They build it up so strongly in their thinking mind that obedience is in all things they do; their eating, their posture, their sleeping, and in every walk of their daily life. They leave room for nothing in the physical attributes and give to them only that which is in spiritual attainment; mind over body.

When they become a certain age, they are changed from their physical teacher as soon as they can prove that they can overcome all but the nerve channel of their body. It usually takes place about their fourteenth year and then they are placed under their spiritual teacher. I use that English term; there are many names that are given to the high selected masters. Many English pronounce them differently. I give to you the word spelled 'gori' and I do pronounce it 'ger-a,' which means head master selected. This great teacher, who has demonstrated he can overcome anything physical upon the earth and manifest many of the spiritual attainments according to his decision, begins the development of mind; spiritual mind, over mortal mind.

The students are told how they must dress and they must clean, or have their body cleansed, by thought. That is why you see many seemingly unclean teachers, students of the gori, as they have not yet learned how to mind-clean their body and their clothes. They are taught how to manifest their food out of space. They are taught how to transplant their bodies from one place to another and the tortures through which they put their bodies in learning all these attributes would leave all of you Americans standing in awe; appalled at the torture through which they seemingly go. You have heard; perhaps some of you have seen, of those who could walk on fiery stone, so hot that the ordinary person could not stand close to them. You have watched those who have eaten of glass. You have watched those who seemed to swallow the sword. To those who watch, you say these are magical tricks. Those who see these things believe it is impossible for man to do and, truly, that is the answer, for they are capable of overcoming the mortal body; changing it into substance that cannot be destroyed. There are many things that take place in the training before they are accepted into the temple of the high priest that are not necessary to be repeated here. I have brought you this much, which I have gone through, and know whereof I speak.

When I descended to earth as a teacher among my race of people, I opened the door to all the training of the spiritual life and began as a four year old child, first-born of the Magnaharro family and I spent all of my teaching years and lives in India. You may call me ancient because, in my last experiences on earth as a teacher, I was indeed ancient, having lived in a physical body for over eighteen hundred years and only changing the body, not by death, but by renewing a body. I could produce a body by the dozens, if necessary, and only changed several in actual count. I have helped many. When I say helped. I stay with them until they are steadfast on their feet. I have helped those in your America. Although I did live here in the Temple, my mind searched out for those who were on the path of life and I could reach them. I have worked with two and three at the same time. They called me their teacher. I did not wait for them to come to me; I came to them while on my search. While being with one, I was helping to write a book to show to the world the many changes and the separations of life and the possibilities of your future. I will help in every way that is possible. I work from this mountain Temple and those who come here searching for life and truth will find it, for there will be many hands to help them.

You call the United States a free country insofar as you understand freedom as it is represented. In comparing the countries of which I am aware, and the United States, you cannot realize the joy and the comfort of searching for truth without the obligations of torture. You cannot seclude yourselves nor can you train your body by torture in America. Your approach by seclusion, your approach by the overcoming of your physical body, is like a heathen, but that is not so in India. What you endeavor to do here is really copying. Your bodies are built differently; your God mind is developed differently; your physical mind with which you think is different from the minds and bodies in India. Your desires are different; your appetites are different; your climates are different, so you cannot use their mode of teaching and have the success of God in mind, not over mind, but God in mind, manifested as God would have a white race manifest. When you translate into English the words of the teachings of the master in India, you find that much will have to have its mode of training changed because the bodies of the American man cannot stand the strain or the constant force that is used by the Indian body. Many of those in India can go very far along the paths of training. Where do you think you will find an American body; that of good common thinking ability, that would permit this change to take place to the extent of forgetting his own race to be another race? I bring this to your attention to say that it is allright to read about and think about what transpires in other developments of religious training, but you in America must follow the pattern that God has set for you to follow. Instead of going backwards to copy what someone else is doing, as this is not the way to find the truth, look at your own way instead of other training, as we say you do not have to go out of the United States to find the truth.

For you Americans who are searching for truth and think you must copy from some other race, we say why not begin at home among your own? I say you will find among many of your Indian worshipers true God in action and the pure Indian would not trade, for love nor money, his contact with higher powers handed down to his race.

However, there are many in India who would trade their souls for a few of your copper pennies; they will tell you they have the magic tricks and they will steal from you.

We are speaking of all this to show you that God is everywhere and, if you cannot find God where you are, you will never find him anywhere else. The only God teacher you will ever personally know is within you, and if you do not open the door to that God-power, you will not find it anywhere else. We teach you from the Temple that it is good to choose the higher path of light; to hold honor and respect for both your path of light and your mortal life; to be filled with cleanliness inwardly and outwardly to develop a worthy temple in which God can live; to see beauty and God-action all around you without making a classification of what is good and what is bad; to find a common meeting ground between your higher self and your lower self as to mind, as the truth will unveil itself within each of you if you are endeavoring to form a program that your mind can understand. If you are endeavoring to fit what you are learning to what you have as education, it is quite possible to learn these things. You cannot group men together; you must understand each has his place.

You are taught here that seclusion away from the world has not overcome contamination, for the very recognition that there is good and bad have contaminated you in the beginning. We teach you that it is good to find silence, that you term meditation, where you can commune with your higher self and find understanding of spiritual conditions. We do not say that you are to live on the mountain away from the world, for God has created all things and, unless you learn to live with all things of flesh and body and mind, you have not overcome your 'self.'

Many of your books placed before the students of the world, especially those in the United States, open doors and channels that would seemingly reveal a mystery. These would entice you away from the development of your own ways and with that I do not agree. What I do say is that it is possible to read as you like; to be secluded when you read and read to understand what other countries and other peoples have developed and how they are using their expression of God and man. Do not try to copy after the method they are using but copy the results of the principles' lives. Look around, over all of the different races upon your earth; your many tribes of races upon the earth, and you will see the ultimate gain they are seeking to find is the same as yours. You are seeking God in you and they are seeking God in them.

In the teaching of the master, we do not teach you that God has classed one thing or another. Perfection is perfection in the sight of God. That which is not perfected must pass through the many changes until it reaches perfection. You will find the grass that grows in one country is different from the grass that grows in another country, but it is still all grass. There are many different types of trees, but they are all trees. There are many different types of animals, but they are all animals. Likewise, there are many, many types of man in flesh, but they are all classed as God creations. They are different in their mold and according to their patterns, but they must come to perfection where there is neither class nor distinction of color or race. Perfection is the God in man. You, as children of the earth, born of the white race, born in this life in freedom, must not seek outwardly for God but must seek inwardly for God. As long as you are in a physical body, the God that is in you works in your God mind.

I would add to what I am saying for your own benefit. Those who work with astrology, which is the off-shoot of astronomy, seldom have the inner sight of truth. They have the indication but not the actual fact. I would give this to you as we have watched you work with some of your charts, figures, and figurations of places. I would give you this to consider: that if you make one actual Zodiac on paper, you should make two that are exactly alike, for as above, so below. If you are going to class your birth on earth as to a sign that would indicate a type that fits you as you are, then you must look at the sign or Zodiac of heaven to see what your heavenly place is and where it is located. The signs of your earth indicate what your pattern is like but it does not say that you cannot get away from that pattern. Many who study as teachers on earth as astrologers, do not see the truth of your earth pattern. This is why we do not feel that it is the answer to teach as a path light of the everlasting. If you have a sign of the Zodiac that you reflect on your earth pattern, how can you tell how mixed that blood pattern is? How can you tell if you are giving the indications of that right pattern? How can you reach the cause of that right pattern? As you go back to the place where you are staying on the holy ground, get out your charts on which you were born in one particular place upon the earth and why it is that you were changed from that place to another place on earth. When you find these answers, you will then find the secret of many things that will not only be a help to your physical life as a person living now, but you will find the answer to many lives in your past. You will also find what the future will give as opportunities for those who are seeking and willing.

This portion of me that is referred to as Emile is destined to spend the rest of my teaching career as a priest in this Temple for as long as America stands. I am one of twelve. Amen, Amen, Amen.

CHAPTER IX

ATTITUDES

June 13, 1930—We talked about what we had received so far at the three trees as we awaited the arrival of our counselor. We were anticipating receiving much more and our wonderment was that we could not resent anything that had been said nor could we not believe it as truth. Although we could not express that we understood it, we thought it sounded very reasonable. We were also wondering if our friends would believe us and how they would react upon hearing that we had talked with beings that did not live on earth. Would they say we were fanatic; would they want to hear all about it and would they permit us to tell them; would they actually think we were just a little mentally off balance? These were the questions and thoughts we had.

The birds burst into song and, with joyousness, began to flap their wings. We turned to look and down the road came Phylos in his white robe. We were absolutely silenced by watching that form. He approached us so quietly; no hurry, no exertion; a beautiful smile upon his face. When I first saw him, I did not see the light but, as he came towards us, the light seemed to flow further and further out from him. Soon he was standing in his usual place beside this beautiful tree that seemed to make the point of a trine. His back was towards Mount Lassen and he was facing Mount Shasta, whereas our backs were toward Mount Shasta and we were facing him. He had asked us to go in silence and this is what we were doing.

I do not know when I closed my eyes, but I suddenly realized that I was praying that God would give me the ability to understand and remember all this being would say and that I would, in some way, be able to be worthy to serve and to give. I felt the world needed to know there were living beings that were not dead spirits. I remembered that, when he had spoken about Christ having risen, I had thought that this was what was meant: That some did not die and go into spirit-land but were raised into beings as Jesus had been raised.

It was while I was holding these thoughts that I heard the beautiful voice; so gentle, so mild, so kind that it seemed to enfold us, begin again to speak to us.

Blessed are they who walk and fear not; who attend to the service of administering angels. Beloved Children of earth, I give to you the greetings from the Temple high on Mount Shasta, whose rays are beaming down to touch your minds and hearts and lift you up from the confusion of earth to a plane where truth is ever free. I carry with me the blessings of the workers called councilors from the Temple. I give to you the greeting of the Great White Brotherhood. My soul greets thee. My heart is filled with love for all fellowman. I shall speak words of truth and give praise to God on high. Amen, Amen, Amen.

It is well that you memorize those words and also memorize the symbolic actions of your hand in giving it. Today I give to you instructions that you personally shall need to consider, for it belongs to each of you and is your foundation upon which you may make your future decisions. That which you call the world about you is not

60

only the community with which you are in contact but you are in communication with all the people that are on your earth that are in human existence, whether they be rich or poor, wise, or sinners. You live under the same vibrations that rule all and you choose of what vibration you desire.

I first will show you how your body responds to the vibrations that are in the ether and later I will explain about what vibrations are. Have you ever watched the weaving that all must use in weaving cloth? There are two shuttles and they pass through two different layers of threads, or cords, whatever the weaving shall be. If you watch, these strung cords are lifted apart as the shuttles pass through and that which have been the upper cords are changed to the under cords and then the shuttles again pass through. If you can imagine that picture, you can understand how, in the space about you, there are vibrations that are ever on the move and are in layers that can be divided. Your thoughts and actions are like the shuttles that pass through these divisions of cords.

You will wonder why, when you can think good, there are times that evil appears. I will use those terms because you are acquainted with good action and bad action. The simple reason is, when you can normally think and your body is composed, that you are able to attract to you the higher thoughts that are in space; they are the higher shuttles that pass through your vibrations. When you are excited, when you are disappointed, when you carry resentment with you, you have the shuttle passing through another layer of cords and this offsets, many times, the vibrations of good. I wil bring this picture down to your very physical body existence. When you are excited, disappointed or sad; when you have resentment or all of those steps which are injurious to man's good thinking, you either lift your blood rate to a boiling point or you drop it to a zero point and your body pays because of what your thinking has done. When you think good thoughts or think about good things or make plans of how your life shall be, and you can keep your blood rate normal in its action and calm as to its temperature, you will find all things will work out as to truth. The same as it is in your body; if you overheat your body, you suffer; if you allow your body to freeze, it suffers.

In your invisible action of your thought-world, you gain

or lose by the attitude you take in your understanding. That is why we have asked you to walk slowly as you come up to the three trees, not to be boisterous, enjoy the nature around you and the friendships with one another. We ask you not to argue; nor to intend any nagging words. The silence of the tongue has much to do with bringing the rates of vibration so that you can weave your thoughts into the right path.

Unless your vibrations can be on an equal balance, it would be impossible for you to understand that which you would call your instructions, your lessons, which will be given to you in the future. We will show you how you can know by the response of your physical body whether you are in contact with good or evil, if you know your own physical body and how it acts. Because you do not see vibrations as you see the lines that are strung from tree to tree or post to post, that which you call your communication lines; because you do not see your vibrations in like ways as you would see the lines, you do not realize that they are about you.

The attitude that we have taught and always will teach is that each man that God has created upon earth, especially those who are the advanced, must do their own thinking and their own communications with God, to be on the safe side. Those who have passed on and who have gained their freedom of going where they please and how they please, can watch the vibrations around many people and they can cause the weaving to fall to their advantage and leave you or anyone else stranded without help. We do not give to you the impression that you have been given a chosen work to do. We do not intend to impress you with the idea that you will be the only ones working. We do say to you that you are far in advance of many who will be serving in the future.

Now, let us understand what I am giving to you in words. By your own choice, by making your own decision of what your future life will hold, you will have the opportunity to teach to many the truth. You will have the opportunity to help the healing of many. If you work as a combination, you can do much good. But, if you go separate ways, each of you can do your work and in the end will see the results. I will show you why you will be needed, as many other workers shall be needed.

A man shall take over the rulings of your country; a man who will be determined that no other country shall conquer this country; a man who will not let the jingles of money attract him away, yet he will mingle with those who have that conscious control of money. Many will hate him; many will admire him, but that will have nothing to do with telling you he is chosen by a higher power than man's choice on earth. He will feed the hungry. He will employ work because it is necessary. Many changes will be brought about in the starting of building of new methods in your country. He will be in the place of decision when war and destruction are all around. He may mingle with those who work for Satan; he may mingle with those who are the devil's ambassadors, but he is wise and knows exactly what he is doing. You are headed for sorrow, much destruction, much killing and much unhappiness. I see that, although you will not take on the uniform of your country, you will serve in ways as yet unknown to you. Things that appear in the public eye to be going one way among the nations, you will find that the one whom they have lent to them their aid to save them from destruction, will out-master them all. It is so written that, as far back as the one thousand years before the Christ-time, it was known. Your bible holds many of these truths that I speak. I hope you will consider and, when I say hope, I am giving to you your own decisions that you shall watch the developments that will go on about you in the next year and that, when you come again, you will be ready to expect the teachings with which you can help your fellow man.

Let me explain. When I speak of these trying times to come and you realize it means death to many, I would give to you a true understanding that on the invisible side of life, called spirit-land, there are thousands that realize and know the truth of reincarnation, incarnation, and the ascension from the lower pits of spirit-land. They have made their decision to come from spirit-land, both in this country and in other countries, to take on the body that will eventually be the soldiers, sailors, and workers of war. They willingly take on the bodies that they may overcome death in service. So, we ask of you not to allow the resentment to grow within you, because God has prepared the way by giving freedom for service. Those who are immediately killed by war have found their freedom and are well on their way to ascension. Those who have had what you term a living death are earning their freedom, if they do not add to their karma, by the suffering through which they must go. We are telling you this; it is the truth.

We ask you not to let your physical mind and body be torn asunder by pity and misunderstanding. When you sit as you are before me, I read your very thoughts. I see as easily as I hear you. What could destroy this country? Why, every loyal citizen, you say, would give their life before they would allow any destruction. You will have much to learn, for brother will turn against brother and father against son because of the belief that will arise to destroy you.

There will be much confusion in your country by color of race. If you think it is quiet in your south, you will find much trouble arising here and there to destroy you. If you believe this one is true and that one is untrue, be careful in your judgment, for I have read the judgment that you have placed about the man who passed over your vast space of water and showed the way for the future by air. Some have called him a spy; some have called him a traitor to this country. I tell you now, it is not true. He has paved the way for your salvation. There will come a time, while it took him many hours, that it will be only a matter of a few hours when hundreds will cross by air. There is destruction by permitting to come to your country what is called immigrants. Those who are passed out of their own country will form a small chain to begin, but this will be the undermining of the youth of your country.

It is not possible for you to picture your future and to know there are going to be times when you will disbelieve the power of God. We say that, if you remember in your darkest hour that God's administering angels are with you to speak the truth, to protect you and to lift you out of the pit of despair, you will find peace. This I would ask you; to write down and keep in record all that I have said will come to pass. Amen, Amen, Amen.

CHAPTER X

FOOD, DRINK, AND YOUR BODY

I give to you the greetings of the Great White Brotherhood. My soul greets thee. My heart is filled with love for all fellowman. I shall speak words of truth, giving praise to God on high. Amen, Amen, Amen.

I am Phylos. I give to you that which I deem is most profitable, that will extend to you a larger view of wisdom and that I may prepare you for the work that shall be given each year you come. I have watched you and I have seen the questions that have appeared before the male mind. How am I always sure you can come each year? With God there is no question. With God, the supreme mind, there is nothing impossible. So, I give to you the only answer to your question that is reasonable. If you so desire to come, God will find the way for you to come. Be at peace with yourself about it. That is all that is required. If you question within yourself the feasibility or possibility, you have put a roadblock in the way of learning which you will have to overcome.

I desire to talk with you today to help you prepare your body that you may stand the test that will be put to all students on the path of light. We recognize that, in your earth vibration, a great deal depends upon the high or the low altitude where you live or exist. There are those who cannot live in the low altitude called your valleys, ravines, and shores close to water. There are others who cannot live, they believe, in the high altitude, some claiming it affects their heart, the vital organ of their body. I cannot go into complete details as to what we shall arrange as your first course or lesson which includes the understanding of how God works in your flesh body. The most important thing to remember is that all bodies can be conditioned or reconditioned to circumstances which are classed as altitude. As you recognize from past experiences, those who live in mild, warm climates cannot immediately go and live in cold, freezing climates. Those that live in the cold, freezing climates cannot go immediately to the milder climates. The simple reason is that disease will come out on the body from the excess excretions that would otherwise pass from the body under their normal or acquainted types of climates.

Let us look at it from a closer view of understanding. When you live in colder climates, your blood is thicker as to quality but not quantity. It contains the secretions of substance that resists the effect of climate upon the nervous system and so you get along very well in cold climates. In changing to a warmer climate without adjusting the substance of your body and blood, you will suffer and, while the blood is changing from a thick to a thinner quality, that condition may cause disease which is sometimes referred to as fungus growth which can take place within and without. Fungus growths do not grow where the climates are extreme in their coldness.

Let us look at the heart organ of your body. It is one of the twelve important, if not the most important, seats of physical life. Through it passes the blood that must make the change for all conditions in the climate in which you live. If your day is warm, the blood must be thinner so that you will not suffer; that you may be able to breathe the right portion of air into your system that is needed for your type of life. If you live in a cold climate, the heart must be able to thicken the blood in order to draw enough of the breath in your body that will cause the heart to pump harder to push the thicker blood through the bloodstream of your body. This is nothing that would astonish your medical profession, but perhaps the ordinary layman may not think that this is exactly what must take place when you come up into a higher altitude.

In the higher altitude, you have less moisture; you have thinner, lighter air and you must be able to breathe twice as much of the air without disturbing the heart as you do in the low valley. In your low altitude, your blood first courses down through the body before it even extends to your brain. That is why, in the low altitudes, it is not possible to think as fast and clearly as you do in your higher altitudes. I would remark here, if you repeat these words, do not get into arguments about it. When you are in your higher altitudes, quietly adjust yourself slowly, moderately, and calmly. Your brain will be washed with the blood first, before it extends downward over your body. Therefore, you are quite capable of seeing clearly, hearing clearly and understanding more readily than in the low altitudes.

Your science makes statements that are true when they say that, in the lower altitudes, the low vibration of sound destroys much that would be good for man. In the higher altitudes, where you are above the lower thinking world vibration, you are in the finer tones of vibrations, and manifestations can more readily take place that seem unusual in your denser conditions.

When those of us who have a finer type of physical body go down into the world, we have to adjust the rates of vibration that we may work within the law of vibrations. It is quite frequent that some of the masters must take on their flesh body and go down into the world that you call your living quarters. Here, in this altitude and in many other places on this earth where you would turn, the air is pure, the water is pure, the atmosphere is pure and the elevation is attuned to the conditions under which we work and we can manifest in a body that we cannot live in upon earth. Therefore, the body that you see, as I stand here before you, is your spiritualized physical body. It is not the dead spirit. It is the live spiritual body that you term astral. It is not the soul but the soul is in it. Likewise, you have the same material body, the same spiritualized body, the same astral body connected with you, but you do not see it. Our conception is to teach you that you do not have a connected God mind and your mental thinking mind. Your mental thinking mind is a mechanism which takes apart all things which you see, hear, and realize. Your God mind knows all, sees all, and understands all. This much I have told you, that you may understand why it is necessary to condition or re-condition your body to save time when you come up here to begin your work. This is the method you may use. We do not tell you that any food that God has created is dangerous or harmful to you. We do not tell you that you must deny yourself of any type of food that you crave or desire. We do tell you that, if you have formed habits about your food, it is necessary to find out for sure if they are habits. If so, then overcome the habits and the food will not harm you. We tell you that, if you deny yourself a type of food while your body has a craving for it, you have not gained one thing. If the creation of craving is great enough, it will assimilate it right out of the ether; that which your body is not capable of handling.

So, the first direction of helping yourself is to follow the craving of your body as to appetite, for craving is not habit; is not desire. It is following the need of the minerals and compound substances and liquids that you need in your body under the living conditions with which you are existing. We do not teach you to become a fanatic and to shut the door against realization of truth, but we will tell you that, as you live in your physical body down in the valleys in the low altitudes below the 3,000 foot level, eat what your body requires; what you crave to fulfill its need. Eat without fear. Eat your own way or style of serving. Do not over-eat and do not under-eat. Be moderate in all you do and you will be on the right side.

When you plan to go into higher altitudes and stay any length of time such as three days or more, you should be able to prepare your body without having to go through severe critical points of change in your heart, your lung action, and your nervous system. How do you do this? It is well to learn the types of food that will take less digestion. In the low altitudes, food is required for a longer period of digestion. It requires that your elimination be normal and flow freely, both the liquid and the waste of the bowels. When you have enough liquid in your body, do not over-crowd it; a quart of liquid a day is all that will be required of any normal working man. If you learn to eat your raw vegetables with what you term your cooked vegetables or your cooked meals, which many of you do, but not always, you may have two or three raw vegetables together and eat them along with your meat or other substance of food and, gradually, this will help the digestive system by ending its strenuous work before you retire. We suggest to you that you leave your fried food alone and gradually get away from it. Plain, boiled meat is much better for you. We suggest you eat fish and foul which is easier to digest and causes less trouble in your physical body. Many of you may question about eggs. We have no argument with the medical science concerning their digestiveness but we do claim that the white of the egg is the hardest and longest food to be digested and to have the stomach be rid of it. Food that is in your stomach longer than two hours is not good for you when you are going up in higher altitudes. We suggest that you gradually train yourself, if you expect to come in June, to eat at least one raw vegetable meal a day. You may change whatever type or which meal of the day to which you apply this. If you eat your meat at your noon meal, it will be out of your stomach by night. Your vegetables that will be in your stomach will be out in one or two hours at the most. You may begin with one, two, or three vegetables and gradually build up until you have a dinner plate that has seven raw vegetables upon it. Use no salt, no pepper or no spices of any kind. You may add lemon juice, if you so desire. We ask you that, if you eat eggs, to have them poached, as you call it, in your boiling water and one egg is all anyone should endeavor to digest. You may eat a hard yellow boiled yolk at any time and with any meal. We have no objection to cook with eggs when they are mixed properly with the other types of substance. We ask you to eat raw vegetables as much as possible. The uncooked vegetable has its own oils and juices which help your digestive system.

We do not include the amount of liquid or juice against the quart of water that is needed in your system. We have no objections to those of you who have learned from your past experience to drink moderately of your fluids that you call coffee and tea, but we do object to the chocolate. The types of chocolate that you have are indeed heavy upon your blood stream. We do ask you, to which you will adjust I am sure, to learn to drink your coffee, tea, or any other types of fluid without sugar, milk, or cream. When you take your coffee and you add sugar to it, you have changed the chemical. The acid that is created is not good for you. When you add your cream to it, it takes hours for it to digest; it becomes like rubber. The quality of stimulates that you get by adding sugar are not good for you. Nature finds it necessary to create an acid unnatural with which to digest foods that you create indigestible. Your coffee should be of the type with caffeine free.

We suggest that you eat coconut and raisins which are cured fruit and they are good for you to eat. Eat of tomatoes, celery, and onions. Learn to eat the raw red onion, not the green onion, for the sulfur in it is a purification and the blood is helped much by it. We have no objection to eat potatoes. You may bake it or boil it, but do not peel it. We have no objection to the small use of your bacon and, while I am talking about it, the hog is no different from the cow; the cow is no different from the sheep. God created all animals. If your understanding permits you to eat of flesh meat, none is different as far as the light is concerned. The only difference is the act of killing the animal when unnecessary. The act of killing, as you call your hunting, is criminal according to your own standards, unless it is necessary for food.

When you become fanatics and you cannot eat this or that or the other thing because you think God would punish you, you are a disgrace to God's principles. Use reason with all things. Now, if you will be able to follow these simple instructions as much as possible, we then will be able to work in a higher order of things when you return.

According to your mental training, we tell you that your physical habits are either going to rule you or you must rule them. When you decide that you are using an excess of your beverages, that is, intoxicating beverages, you close the door to your astral vibrations and you never get any higher than the law of vibrations of spirit-land. We say to you that, if you make use of the nicotine, whether it comes under any name or in any method it is used, that you are opening the door for entities. A master cannot come where nicotine is in the aura. We ask you, when you come, not to bring any of your intoxicating drinks and to bring nothing that you smoke or inject.

Now, let us also be reasonable about how you use your time. We do not intend to control the social functions of the people who live among the earthly types of people, whether they work or associate with them for pleasure. We do not tell you that you must go to any religious organization and proclaim yourself a disciple. We do not tell you that you must disconnect yourself from any organization or church that professes truth of God. We teach you that, if you have truth in your life, wherever you go will not be harmful to you but your life will shine and touch others. So, it is not associating that is harmful, it is how you associate that is harmful.

We expect all students to proclaim the truth of the bible. The only way you can proclaim it is to study it. We give to you your opportunity to have your word explanations in your books that you have in training and apply what you learn from us to your words in your bible and they will give you the truth. We assure you that your bible will give you all the explanations of the history and development of your tribes and races on the earth, if you look for it.

The present now is all you can live. The future is what you are making now. Our only addition is to learn to sing and converse with one another in great happiness and joy. Do not argue; no discussion could ever prove to be true if you have to argue, for truth is lost in argument. Every common conversation is worthy of its place but, when it brings about argument, dissension, and confusion, it is better to be separated from it.

There is no religion (religion meaning to act or acting of truth) in anything where its truth has to be argued , the simple speaking is truth. If, while you go back to your ground where you are living, you have questions that you would need to have the answers, I will be happy to bring to you that which I understand as truth.

We have one more journey for you to make at the beginning of the coming week. We will give to you a journey that you will not forget. This coming Saturday Yessue Ben Miriam (Jesus Christ) will be with you. I will not be here. I leave with you peace, the blessing of the rays of love. May harmony surround you and enclose you that you may be safe from the experiences of the outer world. Amen, Amen, Amen.

CHAPTER XI

WHAT GREED WILL DO

I give to you the greetings of the Great White Brotherhood. My soul greets thee. My heart is filled with love for all fellow man. I shall speak words of truth, giving praise to God on high.

I saw you from on high as you came up the path and placed yourselves in position for meditation. There are many hosts of angels who have been watching on high. They know that this is the beginning of the working out of the many problems on your earth. Shall hate overcome love? Shall nation destroy nation? You realize that this is the war of race, not of your government, particularly, but it is the black, the brown, the yellow, and the white races pitted against one another. Of course, you realize that in the races, the tribes are pitted against one another, as in your white race, one is pitted against the other. Many will be pitted against the success of the lasting quality and the ability of your United States.

The shame of it all is that this coming generation will be so weak-minded that they will be influenced by the importance of the devils' workers. If men could only realize that, by training their own mental thinking instead of being influenced by others, they could destroy that which you term your monetary system and take leave from this problem. You cannot take from the rich man that which he has earned of his own ability; your common sense tells you so. You cannot kill those of wealth and have overcome poverty, as always someone will rise to take their place. Even among those of you who proclaim that they are among the common people; that they could not be influenced by the monetary approach; that they are poor to the social activities as to politics; even these would be the first to rise in high position under the term of wealth if given the chance. Do you not realize that many on your earth have been tested time and time again; that the master has placed in their hands many talents and their soul has not been able to resist this temptation? Some of you stand in the high places again, beginning with small pennies and then your five-cent pieces and your ten cent pieces. All began in a small way and are now in the high places, controlling the wealth of your earth or, at least, in your own country. Man's soul varies as to the action or temptation; what he resists today he may change tomorrow.

On your earth, peace will never reign until you learn brotherhood love; until all learn that they must share what they have, but not for selfish purposes. When all laborers in the fields realize they are capable of laboring equally in proportion to others' labor, then only shall there be a common feeding ground where love exists because there is then no division about labor; only the need that is supplied.

In this country called the United States, more food is raised and destroyed because they cannot receive what they think it is worth in wealth, while thousands and thousands are starving. Your nation, your headquarters know that much food is dumped into the waters of your ocean rather than feed the hungry. Because they lack one cent as to their rate of value, not only in your vegetable but in your meat supplies, this has taken place. If the effort was put forth that you raise as much as your land will permit each year and have a market all over the world, not allowing one country to buy more than was necessary. There would be food, and there would be no waste, and you would not have to destroy that which is useful. If your government was alert to the expenses of how things were run and those in the high places who have command over the services would see that nothing was wasted, they could have the best there is in all of your supplies and not have the expense that is detailed to waste. It should be one of the most serious duties of the command to see that everyone in service had plenty but nothing to waste. All they had that they call waste should be given to those who do not have, regardless of race, cult, or creed. You who feel you have many privileges, as far as your social activities are concerned; as far as your financial earnings are, you know nothing of what the future holds. For you will pay and pay for all that you earn and all that you spend. If you think you are paying for the upkeep of your state by that which you call your tax, you have much ahead of you to learn. Soon, every article sold will be taxed and retaxed and retaxed, until a dollar is not worth half its value. You will learn. In the future, you may make many dollars; you will feel that what is at hand is that your dollar is not worth very much.

While you are in the position you are in now, at least you have time that you may use as your own. Before many months have passed, you will begin to live a life of rush from the time you get up to the time you retire. The spiritual part of your life will be almost the last thing of which you will think, except when you are in dire danger.

73

You are going to be threatened from the east and from the west. Therefore, there shall be one placed in the seat of honor, or command, of your country. He will be hated, despised, mistrusted. Those of you in the common file of life will not see that those who hate him most are the ones that would take the food from your mouth and would place you as fodder before guns. He is like a man of iron and he shall control in his way, not another's way. There are always those who will pass a stone without knowing. He will die, when he gives up his seat of honor, a broken man in spirit as well as body; broken because he could not do more; broken because of the many hands of greed that ruled in the United States, as well as all other countries. You cannot blame the peoples of the countries or of any country, for it is only those who are in the place of making their laws of action. It is always so and always has been, since the time of Adam.

There is much for you to learn concerning the tribes of the light race, but I will not go into this detail at this present time. When you come again, we will teach you what the race of the earth can really mean and what the sub-races mean and what the tribes mean. I do not wish to speak despairingly of any country nor any class of people. I speak only to tell you of what you can expect in change on earth and in your United States in the future. I tell you, you could not conceive, in your mental thinking mind, of what the future will hold. There have been so many changes, down through the ages of this earth, beyond man's conception of time, and there are still many changes to take place on the earth and in the earth and even above the earth.

In this past disturbance, of which you call your depression, it could have been much worse for the laboring man. Now will begin the rise of those that you call your firms or businesses. They will have to change their methods. You are coming into a machinery age where your machinery will replace many men. You will see that, instead of four working men, only one will be required and that one will cause many confusions, until the laboring man shall rise against the conditions. If it were only your laboring man who would demand and plan the change, I am sure that the God of Love would look down and bless them, but the devil has many ambassadors who will come as foreigners who desire to join this country for one purpose. They will sow seeds of hate; seeds of desperation. Instead of the common man rising in high honor, it will be a desperado. If you look back in your early days, there were two types of desperados; those who would kill because they enjoyed it and those who did take from the rich to give to the poor as they saw no other way. They corrupted no one else but themselves. This of which I speak will infiltrate your country, until your neighbor will kill you or destroy you for your aims and beliefs in God. You say, how could this happen to this United States that we love and honor so dearly; for which we would gladly lay down this physical body for the principles that it has in its Constitution? Why, you ask, have we not enlightened the world as to certain peoples upon the earth who have control? They have been enlightened, as we would tell you. There have been warnings from the years way back beyond your memory; from the time that Yessue Ben Miriam walked the earth. It is in your bible. The only difference is in its interpretation.

One man read it to suit his understanding and another man read it to suit his understanding, but the great meaning is there, for those who seek the truth shall find it. The bible gives you all that has been, and is today, and will be in the future. It is so written. Understanding of your country and those who control the acts of the common people would cause you to be placed where you would not be able to speak to other people, if you made public all that you are hearing now. So we say to you, be careful in what you say and how you say it. You cannot be hindered in speaking truth but you are not supposed to get up on the roof of your house and shout it. You are supposed to be very careful of to whom you speak and how you speak to them.

This, my children, is to be the only harsh words that I shall tell you of the future that does not concern you as individuals. I shall stand corrected on the way that I have expressed that last sentence. I do not desire to feel that you are responsible. I desire you to understand that you can be aware of many things about which you can do nothing. Amen, Amen, Amen.

CHAPTER XII

THE UPWARD PATH

My soul greets thee. My heart is filled with love for all fellow man. I shall give you words of truth, giving praise to God on high. Amen, Amen, Amen.

I take you now to the three trees. I see the bowed heads of six children whose serious thoughts are that they shall be able to understand in their terms of life and be able to share it with others.

Beloved Children of Earth, the path before you is ascending, not descending. Do not chide yourselves for that which you have not known or recognized in your earth lives. I have explained that you have returned to earth many times and each time the veil is closed that lies between that part of the dimension you call spirit-land and the earth. So, while you are here on earth, you do not remember the many advancements that you have made, although they are in clear record each time you return to spirit-land. The only part of your existence of past earth lives that you bring to earth with you is known as a pattern, often referred to as the Book of Life. In this pattern is the formula that will overcome all of your errors and mistakes that you call sin or imperfection or ignorance, that you may become more like a Christian man and, when we speak of Christian, we do not mean membership in any organization. The only church that we recognize is the Christ-church within you. That church is your conscience and your conscience never fails you.

Now, the pattern with which you are born into a flesh life always permits you to have an active physical body under which to function, before you begin to develop what you need to work in your pattern. In other words the first seven years of a child's life is put into activity by unfoldment of all the machinery (all the implements which are in your physical body) to work in harmony. The four systems that you have in this physical body require seven years to unfold into activity. Until that activity is at its peak of seven years, your physical faculties do not take over as personality. Before that time, you dwell within the aura of your parents or whoever is in charge of you.

At the age of seven, you begin to function your thinking ability, as a child begins to notice the shape, the size, and the colors of many things, and the sound of noise. All this is known as classification, whether it is human or solids in activity. In the bible, it refers to it as names. Then the child begins to unfold its desires; its appetites. Nature begins to function more into the individual requirements, and after its sight and hearing are developed, the glands of the body begin to function and he becomes known as a man of taste or a being of taste and quality, because his desires must either go in quality or quantity.

At his third step of unfolding his pattern, he begins to find opposition and, between the age of fourteen and twenty-one, indeed man finds many oppositions. These oppositions are the result of the errorless need in the many past experiences and, by the opposition, man learns to overcome that which he had allowed to detract him. From his past, he will have that same temptation even stronger. Each time he comes to earth, his conscious mind is stronger and this ability helps him to be stronger to overcome opposition.

To ask who I am and who I was makes so little difference, as I have told you. I descended from the Kingdom of the Masters which is a kingdom similar to your mortal man kingdom, except that we do not have density. Now, who you were in your past, whether you were king, queen, or slave, makes no difference. Those were days of experience, through which many passed, but what you are today is the answer to what you have been in the past. You can live over the past, if you so desire, or you can advance into the future where new lives will unfold to you the Kingdom of God.

Your problem is to bring yourself to the foot of your master. Your master is your higher self who will teach you all you need to know. Christian teaching is not finding all of the intentions or theories that were put out for many past ages. The duty of your educational program is to teach what is taking place today and what you can expect from tomorrow.

There are those who do not desire to make a change upward in this life because, they say, the struggle is too great. You do not have to struggle to go downward and it is an effort to go upward. It is an effort because you have to leave behind many of the mistaken ideas, many of the ignorant actions, and take on a new understanding. This requires strenuous effort of thinking and, today, man seems to desire everything without effort. As he will, in the near future, be controlled by mechanical things, he wants the mechanical things to also do his thinking.

In our work, as we are explaining to you, we have endeavored to cover the several different parts of the program so that you would not go away from here with a biased view but that you would have an inkling of the past, the present, and the future. We ask you in your effort at home, to meet together one time a week, if you can, and, if you cannot find quietness in your home, go out away from people and talk things over where your memories will recall the words we have said. We offer to help you, if you will come back where we can be with you.

Now I speak in these terms. Perhaps you will have to think them over carefully, but we have several bodies in which we work and you have several bodies in which you work. You do not know your body but we know our body. We will be able to teach you about your bodies and the time has come when you can use them without having to pass through death. Now, the bodies in which we appear, as you see me stand before you, is a substance body but it is not a flesh body. In other words, we do not have twelve vital organs nor do we have ductless glands functioning in our bodies. We do have the systems working in our bodies and these we will be able to teach you of how they function, what they are, and how you can better yourselves by use of them. If you will come that we may instruct you, this body in which I am here appearing is like the tones on your musical instruments. Your bodies are created of more tones, or lower vibrations of matter substance. This body is a substance body and fits the physical world but is on a higher rate of vibration. The substance is pure, without germ-life, and I bear the resemblance of the first body that God gave to His sons of the Master Kingdom. This is the body that I manifest. I can work invisible activity upon the earth. I do not have a flesh body born by birth; I manifested by higher rates of vibration and sound. I do not think with a single mental mind activity. All of the reflections of nerve that you call nerve centers are in one context; complete and whole. Therefore, there is no division of past, present, and future.

All of the Master Kingdoms have an open chart, as it were, for God's creation. I do not need a substance body to carry my God mind, to which you refer on earth as your soul. It is the body of your individual creation of man and that God mind contains everything as to its knowledge, its intelligence, that ever has been created on earth. I would not give you the impression, as I would not be telling that which would help you, if I had not ascended unto God. I have only ascended into that part of the kingdom from which I have descended upon earth and returned. When your elder brother, Jesus Christ, said, "I go to prepare a place; I go unto my Father in Heaven," He was stating words that meant, "I return to the Master Kingdom and there I must prepare the ways, the means and the know-how, that man can work his salvation of overcoming death.

Try to see how much space you can think of around earth and what it contains. Train your intelligence to reach out away from the earth, for indeed, that space through which you look with your physical eyes contains the glory that God has created for man's use, but you see it not. The angels that God has given in charge over you, even though you do not see them, are close to you. To those little animals that you see creeping around upon your ground or close to your camp, if you will look and watch, you may see how God has protected them, for they too are passing through a stage of evolution.

When you retire at night, if you think these trees stand helpless upon the mountain, look and watch of them at night and see how they recognize one another. Tomorrow, when you come, I shall tell you why these trees stand upon this mountain; why they, too, carry out the fulfillment of Gods' orders; why they, too, are under the care of many of the angels. Although they do not speak your language, they also have a language.

I leave with you peace. I leave with you joy. I leave with you the blessings from the Radiant Temple. Amen,

Amen, Amen.

CHAPTER XIII

GOD WORKS IN ALL

I am Phylos. I give to you the greeting of the Great White Brotherhood. My soul greets thee. My heart is filled with love for all fellow man. I shall give you words of truth, as they pass these lips, and give praise to God on high.

Children on the path of light, I extend to you the message of peace from the Radiant Temple. Were you capable of seeing into the future, not just one or two years but as time is measured, fifty years, and were you capable of looking back over those years, you would not be able to recognize all the places upon this earth or your own country where you have been and with which you have become acquainted as to location, surroundings, and the livable conditions where thousands live. As you have listened to our words telling you what will go on in the world around about you, it may seem a far away affair to you, but it is not the distance of being safe from the harmful action of war that is to be of concern to you. It is the effect of war that is harmful and that will reach into every corner of this earth.

When you enter into wars, there will come a time that it will seem like peace and many will preach peace, but there will be no peace and war will continue. It will never stop until the final day, when those that will not live in peace upon this earth; those that will not respect their fellow man as to their own opinions and belief of worship, will come the day when they shall be removed from this earth that you call home.

In my previous words to you, I have tried to impress upon your minds and give food for your thinking of why you were born on earth in a flesh body. Where did you come from? Where are you going? When will the final ending of your going between earth and heaven be? I

80

have tried to indicate to you what is true in your lower mind that you must reflect upon the God mind to find the truth. The God mind is free to all men on earth, whether he be black, brown, yellow, or white, as to his race or color. God is known into the minds of those that are called heathens; not in your way but in their way. Who is to say that their way is not as effective as your way? Only those who find conflict to their mortal way of thinking declare that all else is wrong. God, in his power, understands all; judges not of what man thinks but knows what are actual effective laws.

I have endeavored to indicate to you that, by your effort to know yourself and the reason that you are built as you are and why you are as you are in race or color, you will then see how God works with you and within you. I have endeavored to impress upon you that, if you will come to our mountain place, we will be able to give to you, in form of writing, enough of the knowledge that you can impart it to others. In these steps of training, we shall take the first year to teach all about your physical body and how in it God works. In the second year as you come, we shall explain to you how you are connected to that object that is called your soul; the ruler between the visible and invisible activities of your bodies, meaning that you are visible on earth in flesh and in death you have a visible physical form, yet are invisible to the mortal man. These two bodies in which you work are referred to as incarnation and reincarnation. We will tell you how to use your soul activities properly.

In the third year, if you will come, we shall give you the understanding of how to apply and teach all of the mechanisms that control the contacts between you and your higher self, the Son of God. We shall show you how you can control properly both the visible and the invisible activities of all of your bodies.

Outside of the training of ascension, we shall not follow the rules and regulations of your many schools of training. We shall not condemn or criticize any training that is taught, in your time, that is endeavoring to teach better living and better knowing of self. We give you regulations to guide you and direct you on how you shall meet and converse with other people. This is the schedule that has been decided upon at the council meeting in the Radiant Temple. We shall teach you, as a gift to your fellow man, divine healing, as you term it on your earth and we call natural healing. We shall be able to accept you in the Temple each year that you come. We can not tell you in advance as to what day that will be. That arrangement will be made here.

As to the teachings of the elder brothers, we do not expect to change the people of the world. If you are able to bring through and relay the truth, each of you, to ten people and, out of ten, should bring forth one student of the light, we will say you are indeed blessed. We shall be able to tell you how God's angels have charge over you and we will be able to tell you how they work, when they work, and who they are. For God's laws are never broken on His side of understanding and His law says, and I repeat, "I shall give my angels charge over you and they shall keep thee in all thy ways."

Now, man is not always responsible for what he believes, having been trained for years and years in this life and, perhaps, for years and years in many lives, that God is a being somewhere up above and He knows all, sees all, and judges all. In these instructions that we expect to give, we will endeavor to show you how, by the limitation of man's conception he has very seldom known God. We intend, by this training, to show you God is something that you can know. The door that is closed between man and truth is his ignorance of the laws of God, his misconception of truth and his applying applications of false understanding. I have endeavored to give to you the outline of what is open as an open door to each of you. Age has nothing to do with it. It is your sincerity and desire to know yourself and truth, as it originated in God understanding.

We do not command you to come. We do not demand of you that you come and we shall not beg you to come. You have your own free will. We offer you the gift from the Radiant Temple, free of any earth connection, any earth expense and, as freely as you are going to receive, we expect that you freely give to your fellow man. The roots of evil creep out unseen into many ways and many places, even into the heart of man. We ask you to think, make your decision, and all will be waiting here for you when you come.

Children of Light, I, a high priest of the Melchizedek Order of the Sons of God, come to encourage you to strengthen your thinking ability and to endeavor to give you enough visual action that you can think for yourself. Not that we intend to prove God to you, but we will let you prove the truth to yourself. I do not stand here to tell you that the path is an easy path. We shall tell you that many will turn against you, criticize and condemn your methods and say you are foolish in your understanding. I do not imply, that you will find your efforts, as to your change of living, an easy one. We will endeavor to make it as gradual a change as you are capable of receiving. If you are perfect, you have nothing to give up or to change. If you are happy and content as you are, then you should not seek the change. If you are not satisfied within; if you desire to know more than you have, then a change is possible. What shall you give up? Nothing but untruth and ignorance. You can accept that which is workable and that which you understand.

To teach that which you do not believe, is false. There are many false prophets. To teach that which is truth, as did Jesus Christ, you will lose all earthly connections insofar as friendship and your social activities are concerned. In return, you will find brotherly love; love that is lasting and endures forever. The Radiant Temple, in its service, endeavors to reach out and contact people and, if it is possible to work through others, we will do so to teach brotherly love.

There have been others and there will be others who shall enter into the Radiant Temple and there will be a few who will endeavor to give to the world, by method or word, the truth as it really is. Whosoever shall place a price upon the truth, take a profit and live by the profit, is placing himself in darkness as to his future, for the truth cannot be sold. If man is sincere in his efforts in helping his fellow man to understand the truth as he understands it, then he will speak the truth, he will live the truth, and he will give the truth freely.

Watch the trees as they move and sway. You will notice that they are more noticeable at night than at day. Place this thought into your conscious state of thinking: That this mountain is a great magnetic attraction to the many elements in space that are needed upon the earth.

On the West Coast mountains, as on mountains all through your United States and many other countries, the trees are located in such positions that, as the currents come from the north, south, east, and west; then their elements' proportions are mixed by the swaying of the trees. If this were not so, you would suffer down in your valleys as you would on a desert. So, the trees are not inactive and were placed there for a greater purpose than just to burn as wood. Every tree is sensitive to its position and work. Because you do not understand the language or the contact of the understanding between the two kingdoms, does not alter their kingdom. They must work out their salvation as this kingdom and, any place that is a desert void of trees, is not yet ready for human existence. When God plans that human existence should be there, He will see that trees grow there.

You will find that, on the earth in other continents, there are many high peaks and that they do not have trees. We say to you that Mount Shasta, the White God, is a great mountain that should be loved and sought after for greater purposes than the killing of the animals or the removing of trees. When you return to your camp, we advise you to apply some of the time considering the words that I spoke to you today and you may experiment as far as to satisfy your curiosity. You may find or seek out a tree and sit by it, leaning your back against it and your head against it and see for yourself the connection between the context of the true vibration and that which man calls a magnetic attraction.

Until we meet again tomorrow, I bless you with the peace of light. May it enter into your heart and stir the living waters of life. Amen, Amen, Amen.

CHAPTER XIV

USE OF REASONING

I come from the Radiant Temple and give to you the blessing that is sent from many Temples and from many other masters. They are, as you know, working for the betterment of peace on earth. You hear many strange words of information that come from many others' ways, means, and countries. Not all the good is true and not all the bad is true, but I would say that it could be much better than it is.

I give to you the greetings of the Great White Brotherhood. My soul greets thee. My heart is filled with love for all fellow man, and I give my words of truth, giving praise to God on high.

Beloved Children of Earth, before you entered into your meditation, I watched the passing thoughts that you were holding concerning my presence here. You were wondering how long I had been here waiting. It does not matter, for time on this side is not measured as you measure your time by the movements of the sun. I was not here but a few moments and, perhaps, on the second that you recognize that you saw me, may have been the very moment that I arrived.

I have endeavored, through these conversations and through the demonstrations, that you may see with your physical eyes that it is possible that we can bring things from the fourth dimension to your world of solid that you may recognize and become consciously aware that there are things that you do not create in your own estimation of material things. If it were possible that your mental vision could penetrate the space that is around you and above you as far out as you could see, you would see more in just a short period of time than you have seen all your life in the solid. There is more living life in the outer space around you than there is upon your earth, for, as you have learned through your methods of training or schooling, there is an opposite for everything that you recognize. Even in your word terms, such as using the word love, you know it is the opposite of hate. The word good is opposite to that which means bad. So it is with every seed of grass or any seed of a plant; that its opposite is in what you have commonly understood as invisible but in the invisible realm is the life seed pattern of it. You see the manifestation of what it produces. Sometimes it is what you term a weed, but its opposite is not a weed; it is life and life is beautiful. We endeavor to picture this to you that you may see this physical body of you is only the production of what you are of its opposite.

Your opposite is what you commonly know as your higher self. It is the "I AM" in you. It is the God in you. It is the highest mind of you, but it is not your soul. It is not the spirit of you. If this is true when you think about it, then you must have four different actions for which to account as a physical body. For, if the opposite of this physical body is something of the highest to be attained (the God self in you) and you, physically, are the lowest part of you, there must be an interchanging plan in between. If, when you pass through this change called death and do not go into your highest self, into what do you go? Some refer to it as your spirit, but your spirit is your breath that you draw. It is a pattern according to your build, your stature, your weight, and the pattern of activity through which you must go.

I will refer to you that you have an invisible physical body. It is a substance body. It is called a physical substance because it is like this body, except that it does not have flesh. This body does not die because it could not have disease. This is the body that you commonly refer to as your ego body. This ego body contains the records of all your living activity. It is the root seeds of your pattern. It is the seed that keeps life going and, as long as you create a substance body, it can never die. It has often been said that a man can lose his soul. He cannot lose the soul but he can be lost from it. The only way that he can be lost from it is to cease creating a substance body for the ego, or mortal intellect to grow. When it is, and has become intelligent enough to overcome death, which means you do not have to take on a physical flesh body again, then it may continue on in evolution of growth until it is fit to take on the higher self and walk as God created man.

The conversation that you have among yourselves of how it can be proven so that man can see and understand where the angels are, and explain the meaning of what God has interpreted as the intelligence of the beings whom, where, and how, can be explained but not understandable, in a few words. If we were to give to you the information that is recorded in the Temple about the evolution of man, of past, present, and future; or if we were to give to you the information of the creation of the heavens and the earth, many manuscripts would have to be written. It is something that man is not capable of taking into his conscious mind of the physical body and gather the great understanding, without having the demonstrations, and make him believe it.

Through your programs on the earth, about which we do not complain, you begin your training as early as possible and you spend practically all of your youth in training to believe in the things that you can see and handle, make or create, by your own efforts. But if you cannot change your physical body so that your mind is free to work in the invisible state of existence or, in other words, changing from one dimension to another, then you do not readily grasp. It takes much training and many words to explain so that you can think about it reasonably. We have prepared the way so that it is possible to train the thinking mind to reason out, by word terms or your intellect, so that you will understand. You may be able to believe that which is true and yet not be able to manifest it in flesh or mortal activity.

Let us reason by what we mean in this activity. We reason that, if you have been trained in your earth existence that you must expect the teaching of your bible to be true, that is, the old book of your bible, you must take much of the training to affect this living body that you have at the present time. Now, what do you take as a measuring of intellect? You take the words that have been written that they used in those days, long, long ago. And those that are older than you who proclaim they recognize and believe in God, they have not the ability whatsoever to demonstrate or show to you what they mean. But, it is a traditional activity that what is good enough for your parents should be good enough for you. Life continues on, year in and year out, without any reasoning, until the teacher comes along in your living physical way of understanding and demonstrates to you what God is, what is meant by the use of the term God, what is meant by the use of the word Lord God, what is meant by the word Lord, what is meant by the term Heavenly Father and what is meant by the word Father. Until that wise teacher can come along and give to your intelligence something with which to work; that is, a divine picture within you of reality, there are no words that the bible can give to you that will make it real.

Yet, I say to you, Children of Earth, that, if you would understand your bible in its word terms, you will have the greatest understanding and could direct your connection to the God power. For every record that is in your book that you call the bible, is true. It is the record of the beginning of your life on earth. It is the beginning, going back through all life living on earth. Because you do not understand the meaning of the word terms that are used and because those who teach, perhaps, do not understand (and we do not criticize them if they believe what they teach) that is the reason why you cannot, and do not, understand the difference between the invisible action and the visible action of life. That is why you do not understand the terms incarnation and reincarnation; why you do not understand the meaning of Adam and Eve; why you do not understand the meaning of the twelve tribes; why you do not understand the words that the Blessed Teacher came on earth to so freely give, the man Yessue Ben Miriam, known as Jesus the Christ.

All that we are giving to you here is the demonstration that you can use your own thinking ability without the measuring rod of the theories that have been taught to you. Your own divine mind can give to you the whole truth and this will never mislead you or never instruct you into that which would destroy you.

A great change has come upon your earth among the people all over the earth. They cannot tell the exact hour that it took place, but it did take place. You are aiming toward the ending of your twenty-six thousand year cycle, where a man must account for his time spent. If, at the beginning of twenty-six thousand years ago, the age of Adam began, then you can look forward to the beginning of another Christ son. If you have not advanced until you are taking your place of your first body that you were given with your higher self, then you will spend another twenty-six thousand years going over again all that you have lived and learned in the past twenty-six thousand years.

Do I read in one of you that you are saying, "Oh, well. We have some time left?" If you look forward to five or ten of your years in time, you may be able to reason out what changes you could expect. If your mind can perceive that there are millions upon this earth today, walking, living, and expressing as you, and if I say to you that twenty-five to forty years from now you will not be able to count upon the earth the people that will be upon the earth in a flesh body, you will wonder if there is no end to God's creation. When I tell you that, in fifty years or so there may not be one living being upon this earth, you would say that there must be going to be plagues; do we have to look forward to plagues? I say, no. There will not be that kind of plague. It will be a plague far worse than that. When there are those in physical bodies that believe they have higher power than God that created them, they will destroy all living things upon earth, even themselves.

To all of this you say, "Oh, that is too far. I could not reason that." You have a long way to go. By the time you are arising to understanding of what can take place of the invisible upon your earth, you will understand. I see you ask how this can be avoided. By prayer. Prayer can do what no man's actions can do, if the prayer is from the heart. The heart of understanding prayers are not made by your words. Prayers are made by your desires of intention. If you place your mind quality upon the desires and intentions of your higher selves, that you may mingle of those of that realm, you can do wonders.

Were you able to gaze out into space, I would say you would see strange sights, but your imagination is not able to picture that which is in the dimensions of the individual invisible activity. There are beings in that space that you call myths in your earth teachings. In that space are the angels that take care of you. In that space are the Gods, the Lord Gods, the Lords, the Heavenly Fathers and the Fathers. In that space are all of those who have passed to the other side. They are not dead and inactive. They are alive and active. You cannot realize this. You would say, "If that is true, how can we breathe?" The air that you breathe is not in that space. Then you ask, "If that is not in that space and is not the same as what you have been telling us, how can it be separated?" I say to you, those are the worlds about which you have heard so much. Were you on another planet, you could not see the light on this planet, yet that does not change it. It is the same. I tell you that this earth of yours sits in a solid existence, far greater in density, only it does not have your weight. The very part that you call space, sky, and depth, is more solid than your earth and it turns with the earth and holds and keeps the earth. That same space extends out into the depth that your bible calls the deep.

You can trace as many as seven different kinds of layers of space around your earth and you say, "How can I measure it? How can I know this because I cannot reach out and hold it; I cannot bring it down for me to see?" I say, your mind can go out. Your mind can extend out from you as far as the beginning of the universe, if you so desire. You cannot do it overnight or perhaps not until the ending of the life's span will you begin to find the great truth. It will make you wiser when you follow in your next pattern, if you are granted the opportunity to return to earth, so that, before the ending of your twenty-six thousand years, you may ascend back into that from which you came.

Now, you ask me how you should conduct yourself to make yourself in readiness to understand. If you should come again that we may talk to you, it is quite a simple task. First, I say to you, you cannot join any organization of this type. Nor can you buy as you would purchase your provisions of life. This is nothing that is for sale. The greatest teacher that walked the earth said, "Suffer the little children to come unto me." Now, did He mean that you would let the little children come and you would suffer? He did not. The little children are the little thoughts of truth that come in for which you do not have the explanation until they reach the need; the I AM of you. Then it is a truth. Jesus represented your physical body, your physical thinking mind and, if you do not let the little, smooth, true thought into that mental thinking mind, you will never gain higher understanding. So I say, the simple way to practice is in your home, in your own lives, and with yourself; this will be the most readily agreeable, acceptable understanding that you can undertake. Through this period of waiting, until you come again, let us set a pattern that will govern your daily actions, if you care to try it.

First, you must be selfless. You must never try to gain something that you can use as a measuring rod over your fellow beings. Whatsoever truth you receive, you may give to others. We say that, if you never do anything that is in reflection upon your thinking state of mind, you will not error. If the conscience reflects an error, unless you remove it by undoing it and agreeing with the truth of it, it is a seed of life that you will bring back with you. Never raise your voice unless it is in song or praise. Learn to be graceful and gracious, both in how you say a thing and in how you do the activity as to its conduct. Do not be over-generous, but do be generous, both in thoughts, deeds, and possessions. Endeavor to improve your thinking ability by being a good listener, and thereby, becoming a reasoner. Never form the habit of knowing it all, for no man knows it all. I never request that a student not see good; I am asking that whatsoever you see wrong in anyone else, be it criticizing their words, their actions, or their capacity of living, know what you see in others is what you have within yourself. If you have not cleared out of your life what you criticize in others, you will have to come back and work it out. We say to you what you say they cannot control, you may have a taste of it within yourself. I will explain in the coming days the meaning of habits, obsessions , and possessions.

Wherever you have a good and you recognize it within yourself, it is good to share it with everyone that will accept it. Do not be disappointed when they do not accept it, for this also I will explain. Never allow your appetites for food to become a destructive activity. Eat normal, drink normal, and use proper rest periods so your health will be normal. Never allow yourselves to become a fanatic and I am explaining the meaning of this. When you become so set that you have the only way a thing can be done, the only proper way, then you are lost as a fanatic. Those who say that they cannot become spiritual unless they eat a certain kind of food are fanatics. God has created all foods and given man in his location upon the earth and in his direction of his physical body, the guidance of his guide to tell him what food he needs.

For those who say they cannot drink the warm drinks because it would retard their spiritual growth, they are fanatics. We do say that, if you know the chemical changes of the substances you eat, or the liquid you drink, that does make a difference and your understanding should be the one to guide you. We do not take away anything from you as to your food that your body craves; we give to you the necessity of using the food your body craves. We do say that location, circumstances, and conditions make the necessity of changes of foods and liquids. We say that, if you live in a warm, normal climate, you cannot eat the foods that those need in the higher, colder climates. When you are doing manual labor, your digestive system can control heavier foods that will produce muscles and will produce the strength that you need. If you are inactive and in a higher altitude, your food change will help if you know how to do it properly. That is the meaning of which I will give in your next day's program, so that you will have an understanding of how you should approach the change in your mind. Grow in your mind and it will fit in your body growth.

I will be here waiting, from the next day forward. Amen, Amen, Amen.

CHAPTER XV

ATTRACTION AND HABITS

I am Phylos. I give to you the greeting of the Great White Brotherhood. My soul greets thee. My heart is filled with love for all fellow man. I shall speak words of truth, giving praise to God on high.

I would like to give to you the instructions that you may think about deeply and, perhaps, when you read your bible again on the activity of the man called Jesus, you will be able to read and understand.

Upon your earth among your many friends in your own country and in your location where you associate with others, you find different types of personalities, as you call them. If you were to ponder about this, you would be able to say: He, she, this one and that one belong here. They think alike and they act alike. They talk and do about the same things. And this one and that one over here, they know this and they know that, and they express this and they express that, and they are about the same. I will place them over there and this group over here. Here are the ones that are always chatting about society, activities of pleasure, rounds of acquaintances and going places, and this group I will keep over here. This group is always talking about the abstract things, something onto which you cannot get your hands, something about the meaning of art, the meaning of writing, the meaning of music. I keep this group over there. Through your wanderings of life, you associate through such groups. Each one of these groups you have classified as good, very good, fair, or bad. Each one of these groups you have looked over and picked out all the things that please you, but you have not measured yourself with them and, yet, you are classed in one of these groups. Now, when you pass out of the body, in saying that they are classed this, that, or the other, as you have classed them, you will go into what is the association of their plane or ability, and results of your physical life on earth. When you are in a place that, for the time being, you call spirit-land; spirit world that you cannot see, it is always that, when you go over to the other side, you are going into that same plane with the ones that you agreed, or with whom you had the most activity, as you have not lost, in your mind, the training that the other groups had, either good or bad. This is what is called finding your place in spirit-land, after death.

There are places over on the other side that are called locations and to one of those locations you are going. When you return to earth, you return to the plane where you have been trained. Either you have learned lessons that have lifted you higher or you come back on the same level on which you were in your previous life. Such is the law of evolution of man, both of body and of mind; such is spirit-land.

Now, if a man is evil on this side and he knows no other thing, he goes on the other side to spirit-land. If he has been filled with lust, greed, hate, anger, and malice and all evil activities on earth and has not had any room for God, for his higher self, then he goes to a very low plane of spirit-land, often referred to as hell. If the good spirit can return to earth without taking on a body, so, likewise, can the evil spirit or the departed bad-man type spirit return. If you cannot see the good spirit, as to his

93

individual activity, neither can you see the individuality of the bad ones who return to earth and mingle with you just the same.

I am sure each of you have seen and communicated or been in contact with many that you would not desire around you, even as you live in your flesh. You do not know of how many of even worse character than you have on earth return to, or can be attracted to you, because in some way, you have opened a door. They pour out of the pit called hell by your attraction and they are known as evil entities. If they can find out how to get on your thinking level or get you to their thinking level, you can be mentally disturbed. Your mental activity can attract you to appetites or desires that you cultivate until they become a habit, such as your smoking. It is not the act of smoking, it is the nicotine that disturbs one.

I will explain what it does to all that God has given in you for your use. This is called an obsession; those spirits that do not enter your body but disturb your thinking ability and torment you with thinking desires that, in the end, will put you on their level. When you pass out of this physical body, you go where they go in their plane or level. Many who are called insane are disturbed with this type of evil obsession. Some refer to them as to their imagination ability but imagination is a faculty and reflects what is in your aura, good or bad, constructive or destructive. Now, these entities are the workers of the evil combined to destroy good. They are the creators of war and every evil that is on this earth. These are the workers of the devil, a God who created evil.

You refer to the word God and say there is but one God who created. No, I have never given, in any of the words, that there is one God; there are many Gods. Your capacity of understanding has not yet reached out that far. There is one God that created evil; there are other Gods who have created their division of creation. The God who created mind, the God that created life in all things, did not say it cannot be in evil as in good.

Now, there are also, in the lower realms or regions of hell, those who have departed and have destroyed all the God good in themselves. For thousands of years they have been bound to the God of hell. They watch over those on earth regardless of color, race or person;

whether he is good or bad in his activities on earth makes no difference. He watches for the opportunity to take possession of that body, shoving out the mental mind of that body so that he can live in that flesh body and barely exist as an ego, until his pattern, or time of death, is ended to find his freedom. How do they get possession of you? When your aura is not protected and you find yourself filled with passion desires, appetite desires, greed or lust. When you find yourself filled with hate until you forget yourself, you say it is a lapse of memory, and in that one little second, the obsession can take hold and you are forever lost in this life.

If you allow a man to influence you through the act that you call hypnotism, you are lost, regardless of whether you believe in it or not. You will never be the same. That is why we teach you and all with whom we come in contact, that, if you go where spirit contacts are made, you open the door. We do not say that it is impossible for you to go to where only good spirits can return but, unless you know beyond a doubt and are capable of being a good judge for yourself, we say it is best to avoid that so it will not interfere with your pattern until you understand thoroughly the different meaning of entities or spirit return.

If you are disgusted with the many, many sights that you see of circumstances of living around you; if you can turn away in disgust with that, I am sure you would be far beyond that, if you could see what clings around many who smoke and who drink. We are not endeavoring to make a picture that would mentally disturb any student seeking truth. Do not do harm, do not become a fanatic, do not open your doors for the lower type of thinking life; such as, desiring or hiding your passion or your appetite. If you do any of the things like smoking or drinking to excess, you have opened the door to evil. There is nothing that will keep the evil ones away but to be educated in the true understanding of mind, and to know the true understanding of the magnetic forces that flow in and through you and are about you; to realize that you are the magnetic force that does the attraction. Nobody else can do it to you; you do it yourself. If you will not allow Gods' angels to work for you and with you, you are on your own and can blame no one else for the inter-

95

ference of your pattern.

Now, let us look at the words that we have used as to become a drinker, an alcoholic, or to lose yourself by the desires of appetite of liquors. In every human body created, is the proper balance of their pattern called proper balance, equilibrium, so that a man can think clearly and act clearly, or normal. For instance, the eye is able to judge the proper distance of anything that is from you so as to be able to make your mental mind conscious of what it is in shape, in size, in contact by name. You may be able to take a glass of wine that contains so much of alcohol and it would not affect you to any noticable effect, providing you eat of food. It will act as a stimulant and that stimulant gives more warmth to your blood activity. It will stimulate, if you drink with food, the organs that digest the food and we say to you that this is not harmful. Now we are speaking of those who want a glass of your wine or alcoholic beverages with your foods and we tell you how it acts; it does not act on your brain or equilibrium, it acts upon the digestive system and the blood circulatory system. But, if you desire your liquor for the stimulant you get out of it, that causes your nervous system to be shut off, then we say you are an alcoholic and you are not capable of thinking to judge what is right or wrong. This grows upon you until it is something you crave and must have and you are not capable of thinking with your divine mind because it is shut off. When your nervous system is cut off from service, you have no God mind in action.

When you are in that condition, those entities, regardless of your station of education and life conditions, of the low region can reach out and they absorb from you; not the alcohol, not the beverage with which you have stimulated yourself to cut off all your nervous system, but the essence that belongs in your nervous system they absorb and this gives to them the power over yourself. When you are able to do their bidding, they take possession of you and do the drinking for you, whether you desire to believe that or not; it is true. If you will not do their bidding and you rebel against it, they will cause you to do something that will drag you lower in your own estimation, as well as the public estimation, until you find you are lost to rehabilitate your original pattern of life.

That is the obsession of mind, mental mind, and later, when you learn how and what is the eternal fire, the essence of God mind, you will see how they have closed your door and only you can ever open it again.

Those who will partake of marijuana or the stimulants that change them from one world to another, even as in a dream, will destroy their mental mind and the cells of their brain with which they think. This alone is a complete lesson in itself, of which we would have to take hours of your time to give to you complete understanding.

Lastly, I wish to speak of those who use the nicotine. I will give you a short resume and later, when you desire the lessons, it will be completely covered. For those of you who know your body and know that you have vital organs in your body that are different from your muscles, fibers, cords, and tissues, you know that these organs have something to do with the systems that rule your body. The nearest explanation that will give a quite clear understanding is that, if you have witnessed a birth, you have seen that there is a covering that has been around that body or form that you refer to as another birth, a placenta birth. That placenta has kept that child away from physical contacts with which the parent has been in constant contact. That child, as yet unknown as an individual, has not been in contact with physical substance on the outside in your world and it comes from a slow growth from the invisible world to your visible physical world. Every one of your vital organs are covered with a placenta that is called a sheath. It is the thinnest substance that man is capable of seeing with a physical eye. When you use your nicotine, it attacks the sheath of your vital organs; it attacks the sheath that is around your eyes with which you see; it attacks the sheath that is around the hearing drums, and, when those sheaths are destroyed, you are destroying yourself with a disease that is often called cancer. Cancer is the most terrible death through which a man can go, but that death is the only cleansing that they will recognize and know.

The only way you can help a smoker is to train their thinking ability, unless the sheath has been destroyed around their brain, which is also an instrument or a vital organ. When the sheath is destroyed between their thinking ability and their God mind, then there is no help for them and that is when the dreaded disease sets into them. It has not consideration as to the person or being. Only man's willpower, his own higher willpower, will be the overcomer of the lower willpower to help him. The entities that are around are attracted by what you call the odor of your nicotine and, if their eyes could behold what is around them, it would either cause them to pass out of their body immediatly by death or they would be cured forever. Have you ever seen a piece of decaying meat covered with hundreds of flies? That is the way the entities are about those who smoke the destroying weed, regardless of how it is made.

I have given you short words but much to think about concerning this lesson. Amen, Amen, Amen.

CHAPTER XVI

GIVING THOUGHTS TO GOD

I give to you the greetings of the Great White Brotherhood. My soul greets thee. My heart is filled with love for all fellow man. I shall give to you words of truth, giving praise to God on high. Amen, Amen, Amen.

Realizing that the days of your camp stay are drawing to a close for this year, it is the desire of those that work from the council, you know them as masters, that we give to you much food for thinking and for working out your daily problems, that it will not conflict with those which you have been educated, but rather that it would add and make of all your lives to be filled with truth and understanding like unto glory. If it is found best for you to have, we shall give to you the meanings of your many word terms, so as to help you through this year's preparation for better understanding in the coming year. At this time, I would like to take away from your working mind any thought of mystery, secrecy or individual selection for truth for that which is not true.

Every man who comes to this earth, who is a true Son of God, has a fixed plan that he himself fixed to work out life's problems, until such time as he rises above the flesh and dwells in his astral form which is called the ascension form. In your daily life each day, your own individual instructions are for the development of your plan that you made before you came in a flesh body. So, if each of you will take every day that comes to you as a day of investigation, you can keep accurate measurements of how you grow or of your growth. It is possible that man can watch and tell of his own advancements as well as to know of his losses.

How would you go about this? I am going to tell you that, if you take up much of your time in ritualistic, ceremonial activity, you will avoid your lessons, for, if you crowd out your lessons today, they will be waiting tomorrow. We teach you that, as the sun rises in the morning, that is the time that you begin to prepare yourself to meet the day and all its problems. While you are asleep, your higher self puts into your aura every bit of the vital energy that you need in your physical body for twenty-four hours. If, on arising in the morning, you begin to worry about the problems of the day, you will use up all of your energy in your mental struggle and, throughout the day, you will have nothing with which to work except pain, suffering, heartaches, grief and so forth. If you meet the day with thanksgiving, happy to take up your burdens, asking for understanding of them and follow without worry, you will find that, at the end of the day, you are so vitalized with intense, spiritual energy that life will have become a new adventure.

Let us say that you are like the ordinary type of neighborly people who go through the same routine every day. You rise in the morning and are preparing to go to do your daily work. If you must leave home, you are worried about your clothes and worried about whether or not you are capable of doing all of the work that seems piled upon you. You are going to worry about what you said to this one or what they have said to you. Before you have arrived at your work, you have done a day's mental work and your body has no energy left to finish the day. So, you are attempting to do the work and do a just-good job on borrowed energy.

How do I suggest to you to live? I will give to you a routine that you can use or lay aside, for we tell no man that he must not think for himself and work out his own problems, for this is his salvation. We say that, if upon awakening in the morning and before you have moved your body, if possible, ask the higher self, or God, or whomsoever you desire of making your request, to give you the strength or undersanding of your daily problems and to guide and direct you in how to accomplish this for the good of all. Repeat to yourself that you shall, with courage, meet all problems and will accept all answers that God sends to you.

Now, before you arise out of your bed, you will find, at the end of thinking as I have said, your whole body will relax. It will be with graceful movements that you will be able to get out of your bed and stand and then you may stretch. When every nerve in your body has lost its tenseness, you are then able to absorb from your aura the vital energies that are needed for the next twenty-four hours. If, instead of worrying about what you are going to wear or how you are going to get the money to take care of things, you apply the time that you are dressing in loving yourself, you will not worry. I will repeat to you words that you can think about or use to apply in other terms. Let us say that your name is Grace. As you begin to put on your clothes you will say, "Grace, you are representing God before the eyes of man and all shall see the good that shines forth from you. Only I shall see my shortcomings and I will endeavor to remedy, reconstruct, and build a solid foundation with which my body can work. My mind shall develop in the mental activity to see the greatness within all I come in contact, both male and female, and they shall represent God in action to me."

If you apply such thoughts while you are dressing, you will find a light. Perhaps this will not happen the first time or the second time that you do this, but soon you will be able to see a light extend out and away from you. Look at your reflection in a mirror and, if you can see it, others will see it, also.

If your problems do not begin in your home but begin where you work, if you are working, the first step that you do in the morning is to give God all the glory for successful systems with which to work. In this way you are meeting the problems of the day and, by the time you have arrived at your place of work, those that you first meet will see the reflection of happiness, a peacefulness of ability, and they will join in with you. In everything that you attempt, you will remind yourself that this is God's work and you are working for Him. If you do this, you will do an absolutely perfect piece of work that will satisfy and bring about praise to you.

Now, when you come home when your day's work is finished, you will find it will look like a paradise to you, where before you dreaded to come home. If you work with God while you dress, you will not leave anything undone to meet your eyes when you return home.

If you will remind yourself, when you get home, that this is a finished day of work and that now you can spend time with God as His student and review the day's work to see what you have learned by following or retracing your steps of the occurrences of the day, you will find that the little things that used to irritate you did not disturb you; that the work that seemed difficult before was simply another little job finished; that those who seemed not to understand you before were very kind and considerate in their words to you. This applies to whether you are male or female, whether it is school or employment, and to those that are in your home.

I give you a routine to which you can add or take away as to suit your individual needs. It is an application of applying your mental thinking for adjustments. It is the best policy to show man how he can develop his thinking ability, for most men of today, when using their mental thinking ability of education, apply it only to those things they can see in the solid form. Practically everything of which you can think is termed in the word manufacturing. We endeavor to tell you that, as long as your mental thinking is only the manufacturing, reproducing, or the studying of something that will add to more manufacturing, you will never get out of the realm of mental thinking. All of that belongs to the rehabilitated activity of mortal flesh man and, when you are in old age, you will look back over your life and see many, many days of repetition. You will see little gain and, at the end, there will be many who say to themselves, "For what have I lived; what have I gained?"

It is true that, when age sets in and the mental thinking is alert, that many can sit in their easy chairs and reconstruct the many changes in their lives that would have made for a far more useful life, a far better understanding, and a greater recompense to the change that is called death.

I suggest that, as you all gather together as often as possible, you select a few days and each of you carry out the process of what you will see in old age and watch what transpires. When your mental mind steps out and away from the body and becomes investigative and abstract, then only is your intelligence stretching and using what God gave to you.

Let us see one advantage. When you are asleep and the physical body is resting, your mental body does not go to sleep. Your mental body is free, although it is connected with your physical body by what is called a silver cord. That silver cord is not limited by distance. The mental mind is guided by the higher power and can reach out into realms unknown to your mentality on earth. When it returns back to your body and you awaken, you find that you have had strange dreams, as you call them, but, because the activity in the dream is not carried back to you word for word, you think it is not natural. Because your reflection of intelligence shows signs or symbols and you do not understand their meaning, you put it away from your reality, but it does show that the mental mind is capable of getting away from your mortal physical world.

We do advise any students on the path to be very careful in where they seek the truth. There are many teachers and all of them have some good. If they do not teach you that they can develop your God mind in you, they cannot give to you any power whatsoever or use any power whatsoever upon you, unless they lessen your mental ability. We do not teach you that it is wrong to listen to any of the ministers of your church nor would we tell you not to attend church. If you go and hear the word of God spoken, you will hear good. That which you do not understand clearly is that which you have not developed the intelligence to understand, but it is possible that you can. We say, the methods that have been taught by your many different churches on earth have their place. Those who have counted into the many hundreds of different branches have each found a step that can be of help to their fellow man. Instead of wasting your time criticizing the many different religions, look around you and see the many different types of intelligence, and you will find that God has given to each of you the opportunity to learn.

As you judge the quality of those around you, even as they work; this one prepared to do one kind of work and that one another and so on, so has God made the preparation for every step of the way. Those who come to the place where they can step away from the mental and look into the future of the God mind have the way opened for them. Have you noticed that, for many generations, you had only strict set systems of religion? In the late eighteen hundreds there were words that were written and spoken by those of that time of their new ideas but not much attention was given to them and their new teachings. A new concept of religious systems was brought forth but not many paid attention to it. It is there in poetry and in written manuscripts but, until the nineteenth century, few were aware of the new thought movement. What is new about the new thought movement is just the acceptance of truth. Every new form of that which is called your new thought movement is of the growing God mind activity which has been working for two thousand years.

When you go back to your home, do not keep yourself secluded from others because you are different in your thinking. Do not shut off your friends, for they too may be hungry. This may be food that you can give to them. Do not begin in mysterious words but give to them the truth and do not worry. As you have seen in the past, old friends will pass away but always new friends will come. So the door will always be open where you will find, here and there, someone who is eager to listen. We do not desire that you go back into the world of confusion and tell them all that has transpired up here so that they may become fearful of you and feel that you are not thinking clearly. Nor do we ask you to go back and tell them that you are different or that you are endowed with a power that makes you superior to them. In a few months, you will find many people who will be asking questions or speak of things that have transpired in their lives which will open the door that you may converse with them and they with you about the things that they hold close in their inner minds; the thing that you call heart.

Do you have in your mind thought the attraction of the question, how can I develop? There is only one way that I can give to you until I know exactly whether you are coming each year for the training. If you are designed for greater understanding, find a comfortable place. We say, comfortable because, when you place your body at ease and you can forget it, you can develop your higher mentality and this you cannot do if you remember your body. Find this place of comfort and quietness, where you will be undisturbed and sit down or place your body in whatever position you will be comfortable and find freedom within five minutes. Endeavor to completely shut out your physical desires.

We suggest that you start out with lesser time and gradually build it up one moment every day, until you find that in an hour's time, your body is quite capable of relaxing and your thinking ability will understand everything with which it comes in contact. What it should contact is your higher God mind. Never place yourself in a darkened room; a mild or easy light will not interfere. If you so desire, place flowers in your room. That is acceptable but not an adoration to any certain division of heaven. Include all in God's Kingdom. Do not burn your incense with the idea that you are pleasing God. Do not go before any certain place and say it is your altar and believe that you will find God there because God is everywhere. Seek to find the God in you and nothing else.

The only directions of your position is that, because you know you have a polarity of north and south and that the magnetic flow is from north to south, not south to north, you need it to flow through you to keep you on balance upon the earth. You may call it gravity or whatever you desire. Without the polarity from the north and south poles, you would not be able to walk as straight as you walk, nor would you be able to keep your feet upon the ground. You also have a continuous flow of vibration or energy that passes from the east to the west continually around the earth. We ask, as often as possible or where it is possible, that, when you enter into your prayer or solitude away from your mortal self, to face the east.

If, after reading over all that you have made in your terms of writing here and you follow these simple directions, you most assuredly will have opened the door to your soul's construction. There is nothing mysterious; there is nothing selective as to personality. He who works, regardless of station in life, shall receive. May the glory of wisdom surround and keep you forever in its presence. Amen, Amen, Amen.

CHAPTER XVII

BIBLE EXPLANATIONS

My soul greets thee. My heart is filled with love for all fellow man. I shall speak words of truth, giving praise to God on high.

The light that you see extended and which you have been measuring and about which you have been speaking is that part of the fourth dimension that we, who are as teachers, bring with us. Without it, we could not exist, unless we appeared in an absolute flesh body created to breathe and exist on your earth, but our body is not a flesh body. Your words to understand would be a purified body. It does not breathe as you breathe. It does not exist upon the substances on which you exist and that you know as food. It is possible that it can be made manifest to be seen and heard in words of earth terms because we have the contact with a mental mind and a God mind. It is quite possible that you could feel, touch, and handle this body. I am sure that I would know when I touched your body. I am endeavoring to explain to you that, if I took on a flesh body, the mental body would be controlling the word terms which I would be using and I might not be able to give the explanations from an impartial training. We have endeavored to keep all of this as pure and simple, away from the training of the flesh man, rather to bring to you an acquaintance of your spiritual man. If it were needed, I could reappear to you in a flesh form exactly constructed as your form is constructed because thoughts are things and you can control thoughts. However, I find it is best that I come in the pure light so that you would not be misled and think that I was a departed spirit, for I am now, and you will be, at sometime, a worker in the kingdom above the earth.

Now, because we want you to have something that you can go by as to directions, we will advise you to take your bible and your dictionary. I will take such words as Adam, which means the flesh substance man and is the form in which I stand here before you, the word Eve, which means the flesh body in which you are. The God mind works in the Adam body and the mental mind works in the Eve body. Our next words refer to Cain and Abel. Cain represents death; the dying of the Eve body. The entering into the Abel body is called life. The word generation we take from two different positions. First, the meaning to the creation which means the pattern or formula of creation. The second meaning is the different divisions of changing of the Adam and Eve steps of evolution.

The word term light shines by day is the reflection of the God mind in action. In your earth existence it refers to the forces that control the existence upon the earth. The light that shines by night is the unseen force which is the changing of life and its program upon the earth. These are the controlling forces. Let us refer to when he speaks of the ocean or the great waters above, it is speaking of the space around the earth. In all the ideas and all the thoughts of which man is capable of coming in contact, already they exist in creation. They are things and, when you are speaking of the sea, as it often does in your bible, you are speaking of that space you do not see which is the activity of your thinking mind. You cannot thought things. Thoughts are in space above the earth. In your thinking mind, you are able to see visions of thoughts and think about them.

When it is speaking of the fish of the sea, that is pertaining to the individual thinking, of which each one is capable. When it is speaking of the fowl of the air, it is speaking of the thoughts that are above the earth which belong to the God mind; the Adam man. Now, when it is speaking of the beast of the field; the animals, if you will carefuly take them and read it over, you will find you have the workings of the man's creative flesh body on the earth as to his desires and appetites, to passion and lust, to his anger and his hate. If you will notice, as you read your bible, that all this was created into a formula or plan before the Gods had created a body in which to put them. There you will read the formula meaning the word man and, if you will go farther back into the root meaning of man, you will find it is a formula.

Now, let us advance until we have gone through the words of your bible until you come to Noah. When it speaks, these are the creations or the generations of Adam. It says he begat; he begat sons and it speaks of the years of living and the years when he died. You will find it is speaking of the time lapse which could take you back many thousands of years before one faculty could be developed in a form in the physical creation so that man could be able to make a contact direct with his higher self. If you read those words that are in your holy book, you will find how many begats had to be produced until there were twelve faculties in conjunction to work in a flesh body. Now, as yet, you were not a flesh man known as a race upon the earth, for all this, up until the time of Noah, took place in the ether about your earth, in the body in which I stand before you. It was then God said each must learn for himself, each must have an individual understanding of himself, and each must have an individual within himself. God said he must go to the earth and pass through until he finds God in himself.

So it was that the God JEHOVA created a body that would be of flesh, that would have a reptition of its kind and whose pattern would be different than all else that had been on earth. So, the Gods took the formula for the perfect race and created the beginning of the ISRAEL. Your description in the bible is not to be taken as contradictory as to the truth of a flood. At that time, such change on earth took place, but the story in the bible does not refer to that. It refers to the doing away: the destroying of the old attempt of bringing the devils form into an angels form. Therefore, the Gods, under direction of Jehova, joined the channel between the God mind and the earth man's mind, giving them the opportunity of a return to earth by death; the beginning of incarnation and reincarnation.

So set the law that this blood shall not be contaminated, meaning the path should not be changed.

He gave to man on earth, those of the Israel, a blood pattern that could not be intermingled with any other pattern, because you cannot make the creation of a fowl into a form of animal. That is the beginning of the twelve steps of the development of twelve faculties into perfection and they are called the twelve tribes.

Several of your other words for which you have not found the meaning, we ask you to consider. When you speak of the world, you are thinking of the earth and that which is about you. A world is a condition, a circumstance, a division set apart that belongs only to each individual. When you speak of the word comprehension, as we have listened to many of those most intelligent, superior teachers called your leaders, they have comprehension; they are aware in their state of consciousness but they do not comprehend how it is and from what it came. The division of these two words classifies intelligence. It is such words that you find in your bible of which you need to know the true meaning. Your old bible gives the complete history of your twelve tribes as you have developed in your age, from the time that Noah walked on the earth until revelation of your new bible which tells you what you can expect. This should give you much to think about.

Until tomorrow, when we will give to you the blessing of the Radiant Temple to carry with you. It will be, we hope, a pleasant surprise. I leave with you the light of the heavens and may its seven rays pour down and fill you with the love that God has sent to earth to all his people. Amen, Amen, Amen.

CHAPTER XVIII

OBEDIENCE BRINGS CONTENTMENT

I give to you the greetings of the Great White Brotherhood. Our hearts are filled with love, as the heavenly Father's divine love animates from heaven to earth, over all the children on earth. I am Phylos. I give to you the words that shall be spoken and written. As we stood before these children of earth, the astonishment upon their faces lifted up the rates of vibration, not of excitement but of emotion that stirs the heart and the mind into action. It is the type of emotion that opens the door between that which is hidden by invisible activity and brings to a conscious state of mind a visible activity.

Beloved Children of Earth, descendants of Abraham on the path of life, we stand before you in a flesh body, but it is not mortal flesh because it is not subject to death. Disintegration will not be by disease but by a process of going back to its natural substance without any disruption called death. That is why a master can take from the elements that which he needs to create into form or shape for his use as needed and why he can disintegrate without leaving it behind as if it were mortified flesh which must be purified to be used over again. Because he does not destroy, he has ever at his command all that he is capable of using as needed.

I am sure you have read, through your many stories that have been handed down that you term the myths of the ages, that there are those who are so highly trained in God activity that they can touch the ground and a tree will grow. I am quite sure that, in your mental growth at the time of reading, you thought it was imagination that had caused this story to be written. I will assure you that it is true, as my blood brother shall speak the word and give to you a vision of what can be. There are many that can recognize a type of tree by its shape, its foliage, at a glance. I am not sure that you will be able to recognize by name that which you shall see. My elder brother, Emile shall speak the word. If you can remember it, do not repeat it until you have been given permission, otherwise you may use it wrongly or harmfully and that would not be good.

(I saw this wonderful being. He was so very tall, so very large, that I could have said he was likened unto a giant. Yet he did not seem clumsy nor out of proportion in any way. He stepped forward about two feet in front of the others and spoke the word and, behold, something was coming from the ground.)

I, Phylos, have repeated to you the actual consciousness of not one but all of you children who sit before us.

It was for your understanding that before you unfolded the leaves of a palm tree six feet in height. The astonishment on your faces gave to us the impression that you recognize it as a strange type of tree that does not grow on the mountain. Yet there it stands between you who sit upon the ground and we who stand before you.

(Emile had finished his work and had stepped back and the tree was there between us until we were ready to leave.)

I shall give to Emile the opportunity to disintegrate it while you are still in this wonderment activity of mind. It is quite possible to give much impression in words that will produce a mental growth and that is why we have come today, to leave our lasting impression upon you.

As you recognize the law of your country, you recognize obedience is the proper channel which brings about agreement and contentment. As you belong to many religious activities, or at least know about them, you realize the only happiness, the only peace or contentment, is abiding by the rules and regulations that govern as a body. You realize that in your home life; that happiness is only found when all agree with the rules and regulations that are necessary to hold a home or family together. In the ancient times, and I speak of ancient times as in the years at least eighteen to twenty thousand years ago, the laws were very rigid in all tribes of the people as regards home rule. In most all circumstances, the first male child was always the head of the home, even if there were ten or twelve male children in a family. Only the first-born could ever aspire to be a leader, a server in any of the governmental agreements that were the rule of the country. All others were the subjects and the servers of that country. As this was the ruling in the very beginning of any of the Atlantian countries, in any tribe, this rule existed in them all. When the oldest son became at a certain age of manhood, the father must step down and the oldest son became the head of the household. It was he who gave consent to all things, even the marriages of any one of his family. It was he who set the beliefs, as you term your religious belief, and made of all either good or bad, for all the lesser must be an imitation of God.

In your country, you do not have such rulings, though

in some other countries they do have similar consents of this activity. I bring you this to show you that, out of many strict laws and regulations that were binding even to death, you have gained freedom and, from that freedom, you have the opportunity to look back over the ages past, your activity in many past lives, and gather the results and live according to your desire in this life.

You decided to ask this question while back at camp: Did many, in the ages past, have ascended masters and are there ascended masters among the people everywhere on earth? I shall answer that question.

In the ancient past, although people were involved with much more of the things you call machines, they were more aware of the electronic rather than the electrical appliances for governmental uses which the government today controls. In those times or days or years or ages, there were not the temptations of greed as there are today. For, with everything you have brought over, there is a price paid that becomes an individual gain and, with each one of those individual gains, there is freedom lost. In the days long ago, there were not the temptations placed before the educational program or the people in general that would detract away from the regulations that were imposed upon all as to religion. Today you have your freedom of choice; your freedom to investigate. In the ancient days, man did not need to have that which you call transportation. If he was to ride upon the back of a beast or animal, it was a pleasure alone, not for the need of transportation. Today you need to pay for all of your transportation, so it is a constant effort to have before you something that you can control. Naturally there is the greed and desire of possession.

In the ancient days, when one of age laid aside his responsibilities as the head of the home, his obligations to his own country and government, he lived at peace and ease for the rest of his life. It was not that he could not partake of all the pleasures of life but that he lay aside his body and his life work was ended. It was quite easy for him to be able to disintegrate the body without death that would hold him to earth and he became a server in the ascended kingdom of the masters. This was understood with all who were of his family and of his religion.

With you of today, you are before a world of much activity. You are not shielded from that which is destructive but are given the permission to partake in full of it. Only those who can rise above the material things of life which produce disintegration by death ever find the freedom that is brought about by ascension. In answering your question directly, I say to you that there were many more that gained freedom to ascension in the ancient past than there has been in your present period that is called the Christ Christian period. Man must learn by his own experiences to make his decision to live the life of peace and happiness or to live the mortal man's life of pleasure, seemingly. He must learn to choose between what man alone has said is good or evil. Man has not learned by his application that good has always been but evil is only something that has been created out of it. Man himself has chosen, at the exact place in his life, whether it is the pleasures of the mortal man that fit him or if it is the pleasure of his higher mind and heart that he craves; that his desires are demanding of it in fulfillment. The power that you call God power that has been given to many anywhere upon the earth today among all races and creeds is his freedom to choose that way in which he desires to live.

I shall also answer another question that we have seen written by one of you because it bothered the mental thinking mind of the writer. I read the question as it is written: How can you explain God's love and His creation to be equal among all people, while some are created to live in the wild as heathens and some are given the silver platter to partake of life? Is this equality? I say to you that God has given to all men and to every race the same equality of His creation. How can the white man, and we are speaking only of the root race, how can a man say one race is greater than another? How can you say that God has given to one more of His love in humanity than to another? It is only when you see the evolution and understand its processing that you can realize that God never makes a mistake. There never is that which lacks perfection, unless it is given the opportunity to grow into imperfection.

I shall give you a little something that you may carry in your thinking mind until you are satisfied that you have found a reasonable answer. If, on your earth among all of you as races, you find some a little higher in mentality or intellect, some a little higher as to their living qualities, (as you term culture), some who are able to assimilate that which gives a higher living quality or activity and some who cannot (even though they seem to have the same opportunities) rise above the old conditions of the earth, you will find there are certain things among all races of people that they call good or evil, meaning that they are safe as far as they know, if they partake of the good by the actual living of good. There are others who defy goodness and break down the rules and regulations that govern living of life, and they call this evil or sin. Now, sin takes in a wide margin of limitations. There are those sins that only affect you as a person and there are those sins that you commit that affect other individuals. The greatest of sins is when you or any other being on earth destroys the God life within himself as it is the only channel of evolution. This is called the unforgivable sin.

One more step I will take you. If you can, in your imagination, realize that there had to be a form in which your mortal body exists and there must be a form, a container, for the body which you term your death body, and there also must be a connecting body that is between you and your God creation of perfection. Now you can see that some of you on earth have divided this by the state of consciousness. I would like to divide it a little better for you. While you live in the flesh body that you see before you and you call it your mortal human body, you are connected with your mental thinking mind on earth which rules the two physical body containers. You also are connected with that which is your God divine self. You term it, sometimes, the soul; sometimes you refer to it as the divine spirit of you, the holy breath. The most important part is to realize you have these two divisions; your earthly contacts and your heavenly contacts. When you break that contact, you must take on a new pattern or you cannot be born into the visible body that you call your human existence. It does not matter where you are born on earth in order to take over the life pattern that you have to work out in this physical existence but whether or not you have taken on the responsibility of this connection of your physical existence, as it were. In the mortal body,

113

you must take on a pattern to be born on the earth again but not as a mortal human body. Only back into the human body condition can you be born. This is a stage of evolution in the lowest form of existence. You may not realize that there are many in the white forms of today who had their beginning in the lowest stage of human existence and, when you are in that form, it is the only form in which you will learn of the invisible power of God by evolution. So, you who are of the advanced mentally, physically and even spiritually, you should look back carefully as to judgment.

As we have given to you in word forms for your benefit of thinking, there are four races upon your earth that are called root races. Not one of those races were created by the same God. Those Gods who created those races must, before they can be a part of the heavenly host, bring about the evolution of his races so that they may be freed as to environment and patterns. If, on your earth, you can recognize heroes of your own communities of your religious beliefs, you can recognize that there are things that are in many of your family contacts of beliefs to enable you to see that those born in your family could be angels. For those who recognize there is a life after death, surely you can invigorate your intelligence enough to believe there is one act among all living things to their own creation and pattern.

Beloved Children, we know that you will be in your camp a few more days, although we will not be giving instructions to you. It is there that you will make your decisions of how you will come again next year and it is there that you talk over what you shall receive. If you come, it will be for work, not pleasure, for we will give to you as fast as you can assimilate the reason of why you are on earth, what you may expect after death, how to attain ascension and all of the in between contacts and applications needed to help others. Our blessings are not only with you here but peaceful blessings will attend you in all your days. Some will be of strife for the needs of life but we say to you all that you have lost, or appear to have lost, something shall be your gain in wisdom.

Now, if you will bow your heads, we will give to you as words of blessing the sacred sounds of the Radiant Temple. Amen, Amen, Amen.

CHAPTER XIX

OUR TEMPLE EXPERIENCE

Quickly we had hot coffee, toast and some fruit and then we were ready to go. First we put the camp in order so that we would not feel that we had gone away and left a messy camp. We were dressed warmly and we each wore a heavy sweater. It was chilly but not cold. We checked to see that everything was in order and lined up to start our hike, with Jerry in the lead and Bill bringing up the rear.

We each had our lunch tied into a pillowslip and it consisted of fruit juice, tomato juice, onion, hard boiled eggs and sandwiches. We carried a lemon in our right hand. We each had a walking stick and called it our wand. We carried toilet paper to put on the leaves of the trees, at the suggestion of the Forest Ranger, so that we could find our way back to camp. He told us that birds would not bother this, as they would string, and to hang it at head level so that it would be easy to see and find later.

A few minutes before 5:00 a.m., we started up the trail. We had been cautioned not to hurry but found ourselves soon at the three trees. Evidently, we had been walking fast, as we were quite warm. We stood there and looked around at the valley which was clearly outlined, even though the sun was not yet risen. Then we started on the high climb. As yet, none of us had been up on the mountain, except for riding around the trails in the car, and it was a long, tiresome walk. We were weary by the time we had reached the tree line.

We decided to hike for twenty minutes and then rest for three and that no one was to go more than five feet in front of the other. We climbed over large rocks to get through a stream bed and it was a strenuous task. We began marking trees at the beginning of the forest. As we entered into the trees and had gone some distance, we looked back and could see the path exactly where we had come. We had been told to keep going to the east until we reached the ridge and this was our effort.

Finally, we came out into a patch that was like paradise. It was a meadow with beautiful wild flowers blooming. At the edge of the meadow there were two fallen trees that were perfect, upon which we rested. We sat there and talked and rested for about twenty minutes and by then it was about 9:00 a.m. We then began our climb up the ridge, going slower and resting more often.

We kept climbing on the ridge until Jerry finally said, "I see ahead, outside of some taller brush, two trees. I believe that this is where we are to rest and eat our lunch." We climbed for another half hour and came to the two little trees. On this part of the ridge, grass was growing and it was a different kind of grass than I had ever seen. There were other trees around but they were not like the two pine trees. I cannot tell you what kind they were but they were certainly bent over and wind-blown. From where we were standing, we could see over the ridge that led down to Mud Creek. We sat down and could only see the top of the trees down below and they hid most of the hills and buttes. The sun was shining on the snow that was still up this high on the mountain and it was so beautiful; shining just like a diamond. Jerry looked at his watch and it was exactly twelve noon. We were told that we were to eat our lunch, rest and then start back down the mountain at 2:00 p.m.

We ate our lunch and lay down to rest, Jerry putting out his arm so that I could rest my head upon it. He was saying to me, "I feel this is a most blessed day of our lives. I am so glad that we are together to share it." I could not see his face, so I raised to a sitting position to see into his eyes. They were so beautiful as he had these great emotions of truth coming through him. As I sat back, I looked across at a massive rock that was about twenty feet away from us. It seemed that the rock moved and my first thoughts were that the altitude was affecting me and that I had better lie down.

Soon I knew what was happening, for part of the rock turned as if it were on a pivot and in the opening stood a beautiful being. It was not Phylos. I did not know who it was. I grabbed Jerry and pointed. He sat up and all the others sat up because they knew something was happening. This beautiful being extended his hand toward us and said, "Welcome. Come and enter."

Without stopping to wonder, we entered. We stepped into a brightly illuminated room, so bright that I thought the sun must be shining in from somewhere. From somewhere came a great light that was not the sun and it so illuminated the room that we could discern every crevice in the walls. When I turned to look at the door it was closed and I realized the outside world was gone. The opening through which we had come was gone and I panicked. We were intelligent people and had entered a cave and were closed within it, swallowed up from the world. They would never find us; they would never know what had happened to us. All this was fleeting before my mind's eye. I could see my mother's grief. I was sure many friends would wonder what had happened to us.

Then I heard a voice. "I am the keeper of the door. I am Calvita. Come and be seated." This being pointed toward the center of this great, massive room and in the center was the longest table I had ever seen. It seemed to be of a beautiful marble. I am not familiar with the different types of marble but I saw that this table of marble had no dark in it. It had tones of pink and blue and gold flakes with a pattern that seemed to be like leaves through it. When I looked at the end of the table, I saw Phylos sitting there. He said, "Come my Children. Find yourselves comfortable places."

I looked at the walls, trying to find the source of light and wondering from where the light was coming. There were no openings and I did not see the sky. The walls seemed to be made of gold, or that is what I thought. Here we were, in a cave where gold was trimming massive stone and rocks. I had never seen a gold mine and did not realize that this was not possible. The being who had invited us into this cave, whose name I could not remember, was still there and so was Phylos, but I saw no one else. There was faint and far off music, as if a pipe organ was being played, but I saw no place where it could be. I noticed the quietness of Phylos. I did not realize that the illumination that was around him was different or that it was different from that which was on the walls and filling the cave. I wondered how they had ever gotten such a massive table up on the mountain and if they had to carry it piece by piece and then put it together.

Then a voice said, "Welcome, Children of Earth,

guests of the Radiant Temple. Yes, we will permit all to call it a Temple, for this is where we work. Those who come from the Master Kingdom would come here first and we make the change of our body so we may work upon the earth. Yes, this Temple has the door that you saw open but not many feet of the earth enter. We have permitted you to come here, that you may know your guardian angels work for the good of man; that his understanding of God may be illuminated in his life quality so that he can become the Son of God. Strange things may happen here that you will not immediately understand but we would impress upon you that your past lives are real and they are a part of you that you can never lose. Your future life can become a changed pattern at your earth will."

While he was talking, I was looking at the table. Strangely, the table seemed to be moving like there was an ocean wave upon it. In miniature form, I began to see life. As each crest of the wave came towards me, I saw many changes and somehow I knew it was me. Some scenes were not pleasant to see and there were others that I wondered how it could be so. I heard Phylos say, "These are the patterns of life you have lived as you have evolved toward Godness." I knew he kept talking but I was aware only of the changes in the miniature forms that I could see coming towards me on the table. At last I saw a recent life, one before this one, and I recognized it was happening in the United States in the very beginning of its time. I saw my babe in my arms as we were killed by Indians and I saw the cabin in which I had lived. I knew death but I also knew freedom. I knew that I had helped to build this country. Somehow, I felt I should have been more than I am today from the experiences through which I had passed and that, because of them, I should have been helped to live at a higher standard of life.

I looked up and saw beautiful smiles on the faces of all. Phylos said, "Yes, my Children, these are the stepping stones of your life. We have brought you to this mountain. We sent Aftna, our messenger, to prepare the way that you should come here to find out the truth of life and the purpose of God in man. Man has the opportunity on earth to learn the pattern of his life that he came here to finish. God is a reality; it is only man that is not reality in a physical body. Yes, you are still in your physical body but, as you climbed the mountain, your bodies were purified by your obedience. This cave, as you term it, we call the Radiant Temple and it has been here for thousands and thousands of years.

"We are giving you the opportunity, in this year's work, to lay the foundation for that which you will learn. We are asking you to become teachers. We do not expect that you will go back among the people where you live and astonish them with the mystery of the mountain, as that is for you to hold special, but we do ask you to teach them the truth of life. We shall give to you in simple language so all will be able to understand.

If you will come, not because we ask you to come, but because you desire to come the first of June of each year and spend thirty days, we shall teach you the truth of life. We shall teach you who God is and whom God represents. We will teach you the truth of the bible. We will take from the truth of life any magic appearance that may appear to be and give to you life in reality. We never command or demand of anyone to serve. We give to each that opportunity. Responsibility is the only command that can be received and that is given from the heart.

"How can you think of God as being just and kind and equal to all if He could favor some and cause others to be in low places? God is love, but you must understand what love is."

Then I looked up and all around the room against the wall were standing forms. Oh, how they appeared to shine so differently from we of the human being. I saw Phylos raise his hand and he said, "Escort the two men to the inner room." Two beings approached. Their robes were exactly alike and one had a blue scarf over his shoulder and the other had one of green. They seemed to be so white and pure; they were beautiful. One came on the side of the table to Jerry and took hold of his arm, assisted him to stand and the other did the same to Bill. Then I saw them walking toward the other end of the room from which we had entered. I was so astonished that they would be taken someplace where we were not permitted to go. We had not been invited and no one approached the females; no form approached the table where we sat. I wondered as I had never been left behind

119

before. I was always right beside Jerry.

I was thinking that I might never see Jerry again. What should I do? I looked at Leona and she did not seem surprised. I looked at the girls and they seemed satisfied. They did not think that it was strange that the boys would be taken away from us. I looked at Phylos, ready to ask, "What do you mean, to take the boys away?" On his face was a most understanding smile. It just seemed to radiate peace and calmness. I heard him say, "Beloved, it is not because you are not worthy that you have not been permitted to enter the other chamber. No female body in physical form has ever entered in the inner chamber. It is only a matter of understanding that the male body of physical form can stand higher readings without danger to their mental bodies than the female body. The simple truth is that they enter into their higher body where they may be able to see out over the world; this universe that surrounds the earth, and into space and depth. When they have finished in their instruction, they will return in that body because their male bodies can stand the rate of vibration and return into their flesh body. While the female body is constructed to a finer rate of vibration, they could not make the change for, if they left their physical body, they would not be able to return into a flesh form."

I was more calm, more content, and I heard his voice continue.

"This is a particular type of rock. It is not gold; this that you see as gold is the reflection of the illumination that is in the Temple at all times. There is no opening to the outside and, although we do not have a window, as you were thinking of fresh air, there is pure air in here."

How long we sat there and waited, I cannot say, but soon Jerry and Bill returned. Both of them had been weeping. They were both escorted to the side of the table on the left side of Phylos and there he admonished them by saying, "Tell not one word to those near to you in confidence nor to strangers what you have witnessed in the Inner Temple. We ask you not to vow or swear that you will not disclose this that you have seen, but we say to you that, when you believe firmly in God, in you will rest His secret that it is not time to reveal."

While he invited them to be seated again, I was

thinking within myself, "I will get the secret. I will know. Jerry will tell me." How little I knew Jerry, for, until his death, he never told me one part of that secret.

Phylos said, "Now, I will be with you at the three trees tomorrow. Those who have led you into the Inner Temple are Mol Long and Emile, and they will help you to learn the many things in these coming years to prepare you to put before the public or the people with whom you come in contact, the truth as revealed on Mount Shasta in the Holy Temple. You will return now to your trees and pick up your sweaters and put them on, regardless of how warm you seem to be, and immediately start back to your camp. We advise you not to rush down but to keep a steady pace. You will be very tired and hungry. I suggest that you eat fruit and drink liquid and have a campfire going in silence only."

I noticed that there seemed to be an outward glow and I turned toward that end of the room and the door was open. That beautiful being was standing there. I could see the sunshine and what a difference in the light within and the light without! There was no comparison.

I realized that somebody had taken hold of my arm and was helping me to rise. I was escorted to the door by whomever it was that had their hands under my elbow. The smile on the being at the door was the assurance of welcome and the pleasure that had been while I had been there. When we were on the outside we were all quiet and sincere people.

As we stood around the campfire that evening, I, for one, was thinking, "How could I ever tell anyone else that had never been up here what is here and what has happened? How would I help them to understand, for I, myself, was not sure I understood."

This was the most outstanding day of my life. Each agreed that they had never dreamed anything like this could exist. This was June 17, 1930.

CHAPTER XX

WORDS FROM JESUS CHRIST

Beloved Children, you who have come on this side of the mountain and have found what so few have been able to find; a path to the Temple. Although I was in the Temple when you came and entered into it, it was my elder brother's priviledge to welcome you there. Yes, I have come on earth, also in my divine body in which I have appeared many times, to work through the many years between the times I have appeared in flesh.

The account that you have of my life and existence upon your earth is most important to you. At the time I appeared as a son of Joseph and Mary, you at that time referred to me in your records as Jesus and Christ. In your record that you call the history of the life of Jesus the Christ, you give an account of the birth of the son of Mary and Joseph and you picture it as a child born in a stable, lying in a manger among the animals as they ate. Mary and Joseph were fleeing their country that I might be saved. Then you continue in your history records that I grew up as most children of the times, learning my father's trade and getting little education, as that was all we could afford, for in those days much travel was needed to secure the use of the educational program. It is said that, at the age of twelve, I was able to converse with the higher priests and that they considered me wise. From there on they give an account with a vague description of places of living until I became, at the age of thirty, a man who began to preach salvation to man.

Of course, you have read all of these records, and through the years that you have been taught by your religious programs, you have endeavored to believe it. You, like many others, have found the many little partings of the ways that would coincide with truth. Although you would not come out and deny it, you would not affirm it. I would not be here to change your opinions, if they were true. I would not be here to change any true historic records, if they were true. All of these little formalities that you have built up around the life of Jesus the Christ, both at His birth and crucifixion as well as His ascension. If they were true, I would not say one word.

The place that I was born was not in a manger nor a stable. It was when my father and mother were traveling that I was born. My name was not Jesus as a given name, my name was Yessue. My father's name was Joseph Ben Miriam. He was a carpenter by trade.

The word Mary means mother of pure truth. The word Joseph means generation of truth, Sons of God. The word stable refers to the mortal flesh body; the word animal is the house of the animal body. The word manger means the pattern of your life or the program that you must work out. Now, the hiding away, or the effects of having to travel from one country to another, had the meaning that, when the flesh body was born, you traveled away from your higher self.

Now, if you will study your ancient script, where all of your intelligence as to languages have their meaning, you will find, for example, the word God had many different tones that you call pronunciation of vowels or consonants in language. So, likewise, does the word Jesus and the word Christ refer to different activities of one man, each of you as one man. The word Jesus refers to your mortal conscious mind, which is in your flesh body, and the word Christ refers to the Christ consciousness, which has its connection with all mortals who have not disconnected themselves from their soul. It was intended, at the time the records were made of your bible, to give all of this in description but, because of the time and condition, many were forced to hide their truths. The one country or class of people who had the truth, hid these words and descriptions upon which many religions were founded. The truth was hidden to some and yet plain to many.

The whole life of the man called Jesus the Christ is symbolic. There was a man who walked the earth in the life that reflected Jesus the Christ, but the many activities that would express the truth and explain it have been left unsaid.

By your records as given, you know and realize that there was much travel to distant places. In many of your records, you would be carefully kept away from your ocean waters where much travel extended north, south, east, and west. It did not cover the time that I traveled northward up the coast of your eastern continent, the west coast of it, to the islands far to the north. It did not give you the records of the types of trade that those of my family, both on my mother's side and on my father's side, conducted in one country to another or into one race to another. These records also say I have been a Jew. As far as the Jew is concerned, if you wish to call me Jew, I am not a Jew as to race. I am not a Hebrew, as far as my race pattern is concerned, it has been through many different types of patterns called your races upon the earth. I have always been a Son of God and, until you know the real, true meaning, you cannot understand what it means to be a Son of God. I am not continuing to give you the rest of my life as I lived it in the body called Jesus the Christ arisen. I have given you this much that, if you are anxious to know all truth, you will seek to know all truth and, if you find out all truth of which I have represented, then you will have the key to your salvation. This I taught while I was Yessue Ben Miriam and the twelve disciples taught it, even the Jew who took that which you say is a price; you must understand that also.

Now, let us return and say that I who lived on earth that you refer and know as being Jesus the Christ the son of Mary, a virgin, and the son of Joseph, the father of Jesus, let us refer to them as your state of mind that you use as faculties. Your five senses, with which you have been born in your physical body, develop and become aware of all things that exist upon this earth. Joseph is the Christ faculty and the father of your God mind that contains the faculties of wisdom which truly are the Sons of God. It is impossible to put the use of your faculties in physical things upon the earth but it is possible to fit the earth intelligence of your five senses to conceive and perceive the activities of the God mind with which you work but do not see on your earth. It is said that I have left a pattern that man could follow and then he would be known as a Christian that is taken from the word Christ-ness. If he would follow these patterns, he eventually would find a beginning of his life in freedom and he would never be bound again to earth.

It is said that the ten commandments that Moses left

were a stepping stone to Christness but there were not many that followed. I have left in the records of the Christness in Jesus many records for use of the commandments and these laws have not been lived too closely. Therefore, much of the attainment has not been gained. I have said "love thy neighbor as theyself", love that includes all forgiveness, kindness, mercy, patience and understanding, but not harmfulness, but so little of it is used that not much improvement has been made. So, generations of man will find a change on mother earth which makes many changes as the period of time goes on in its writing. There comes a time that, when man will not save himself, nature forces him to make a change called death. There comes a time in his spiritual life when he will not follow the pattern and learn for himself and then the natural laws of God's Kingdom will force him to make a change.

It is said I came to earth to show man the way of salvation by overcoming death, but man has misinterpreted again the meaning of the word death. He has felt that death is something that separated man from his body and he dreads the time to come. A man that has clear thinking ability knows there is so much to be done to clear his pattern of life and he often recognizes when death comes near that he has not cleared his pattern. However, that is not the meaning of the word death. Death means disintegration, not only of the physical body, but of the pattern that man has taken on to work out. For those who will not believe in incarnation and reincarnation, they have lost the connecting link of the long chain and, until they are able to mend that link and join the chain, they have lost the ability to ever return to the Sons of God's Kingdom. Death is the meaning of the broken chain.

It is planned that, if you will return to these mountains, we will find a way to bring you to both understanding of the past to the present and show you what the future will be. Because of the great misunderstanding by your word terms, it must be taken apart and set together correctly. But I leave you with these parting words that you may carry with you when you go into your valley home.

Walk with your head high and your eyes upon the

space above you. Seek to know and understand that space, for in that space are the dimensions of which you are not aware.

It is not what you join or to what you sign your name that makes you a Christian. It is not what you shout nor tell others what you are that makes you a Christian. A Christian is living peacefully, acting kindly and gently, being merciful and not criticizing, or being the judge of what is right or wrong. Learn to know the meaning of justness of self and the purpose of being selfless as to personality, but be purposeful as to your personality. Be able to look upon those things that you call sin and evil as the yardstick of measurement needed for learning. There is no Christness unless you have it within you so that you are able to see it in others. Until you understand that you are the Christ within that Jesus body, you will never know the true meaning that God has blessed you and given you to be the Son of God in a Christness that is in this Christ Jesus body. When you have found those steps to be true within, you will ascend and you will find the meaning of the cross and the persecution. You will find that, in the meaning of healing, is salvation to man.

I bless you, my Children, with the love of my mother. I bless you with peace. May your days that you walk upon the earth unfold the truth of the Christness in each one of you. Speak the words of truth and they shall live long after you have laid aside your Jesus body. I will always be close at hand. Amen, Amen, Amen.

CHAPTER XXI
LESSON FOR INTROSPECTION

Greetings to all Seekers from the Great White Brotherhood. My Soul greets thee. My Heart is filled with Love for all fellowman. I shall speak words of Truth. Giving Praise to God on High.

It is time to make use of your knowledge of how to become Spiritual in your daily actions. For those who desire to gain greater and better Spiritual Understanding, it is good to have the right meaning for the words as used here, "becoming Spiritual". Perfection is the word for Spiritual living. Some may desire to fit the word Christian for the word Spiritual, it would be all right for they have the same meaning. I am sure no student would say or believe that he was perfect, yet we must be sure lest we find the student is VAIN. The Great Teacher that you and I have heard so much about, Jesus the Christ, said "Why callest me good, none are good". In this meaning, He was telling those who followed Him, listening to His words of Wisdom, that the effort of being good was not an easy task, nor seldom brought about any triumph. This Great Teacher led them on to keep trying. Each time they passed through MISTAKES or EXPERIENCES, it made it easier for self understanding.

In this lesson we shall begin to find the failures and mistakes, and if you are willing, we shall do something about them. Then you will gladly give your time to STUDY THE CAUSE of them. When you can see the difference in your work, in your home, with your family, among your friends, and in yourself, then you can realize that you are changing for the better.

We will begin with RETROSPECTING: This word refers to looking backward through your time of life actions. Here are instructions for you to follow. Take one day at a time until you are sure that you can see the way you are to follow. In this way you are going to do something about your life pattern.

If you think you do not need this help, that you already have much work to do, then think about others who may need your help. Do something about helping them to understand. If you are in need of SELF UN-DERSTANDING, then here is your opportunity to help yourself, and to be more eager to help others.

To begin to study, find that part of a day or evening you can have for a quiet study period. Think about YESTERDAY, your last day, while the records of the day are fresh in your memory or mental thinking mind. We will begin to compare the records to the Picture of Questions and Answers, which will be used for study work. Have a loose leaf tablet to keep your records that you will make of every hour of your past day. Record all the happy occasions and the unhappy events that occurred during the day and these are what you will study. Your memory may not be good, and if you write all these things down now, you may review them when you need them most.

Instead of this lesson pointing out to each of you how to learn about yourself, I will let you look as it were, into a looking glass and watch what is going on. In the record shown, you may pick out what you wish to use. In this picture forming, there is nothing per-sonal, and no one can be offended. The object of this study is to point out what causes disturbed sleep and ill health. As you have so often heard the words, "As a man thinketh, so he is", I am sure that you will agree that these words are true.

I will begin by telling you, this person, the looking glass IMAGE, has had many good days. Everything seemed to go along perfectly. There were also bad days and everything seemed to go wrong. All the things that have happened throughout the day are fresh in the mind, or memory, leaving upon the face the reflections showing happiness. The moments of unhappiness or sadness have left their marks of painful moments upon the face also, and these are the wrinkles of old age.

I shall ask this IMAGED PERSON questions, and I shall answer these questions so that you will have the records for your study work. Question: Were you un-happy yesterday? Answer: Yes I was unhappy yester-day!

COMMENT: Unhappiness is a mood. It can be-come a habit. The mood of BEING SULKY, the mood of UNCONTROLLED TEMPER, the mood of LAZI-

128

NESS, the mood of RESTLESSNESS, and the mood of UNREASONABLENESS, are the emotional mental habits of your daily life. Unhappiness comes with the use of one or more of these habits. You may think that you do not use these habits, but if you will patiently keep the records, you will know for sure if you have been using any of these habits.

SULKY MOODS can cause a mental retardment. UNCONTROLLED TEMPER will bring on fever and this may lead to stages of fits. The mood of RESTLESS-NESS, shows a mental lack of calmness, and shows a disturbed conscience. With loss of sleep, this can cause a nervous breakdown. UNREASONABLENESS as used, often brings about indigestion and ulcers. LA-ZINESS brings on a careless personality and makes a sluggish thinking mind. This will also slow the action of the digestive system.

My next QUESTION: Did you have your feelings hurt yesterday? ANSWER: Yes, someone hurt my feelings yesterday, may I tell you about it? I had unkind words said to me, by a person I had high regard for. I was so offended by what was said to me, I wanted to say something back that would hurt them in the same way. I was so hurt, I could not think of what to say, so I just stared at them. Then I got Angry and Indignant, and I never want to be around them again.

NOTICE: All this thinking was going on in the mental mind. COMMENT: All three things took place in this word action, ANGER, INDIGNATION and REVENGE. There was THOUGHTLESSNESS and UNKINDNESS on the part of one person, and on the other side you have HURT FEELINGS. To AVOID, to Escape is the last emotional thought held.

ANGER causes one to JUDGE and in the emotional feeling there cannot be clear thinking. Results are headaches, fast pulse and heart pains. To be INDIG-NANT shows an obstinate disposition. Reasonableness is impossible, until time has quieted them down, or until they have time to talk this out of their system. The THINKING has already set in action through the work of the GLANDS, CHILLS and FEVER, to take their toll. To DESIRE to hurt another for what had been done to them is, REVENGE. Revenge brings about in the body

129

Arthritic and Rheumatic trouble, and so much pain to bear. Last is the thought of AVOIDING this person. You cannot overcome any trouble by not meeting it and overcoming it. To let another person know that you are avoiding them, only opens the door for the same thing to happen again. Meet this person with a BIG SMILE. I do not mean something that appears to be a sneer, but a smile that speaks of friendly forgiveness. I assure you they will love you deeply, for God is in them as much as God is in you. The hurt feelings, if not controlled, leave a very DEPRESSED MIND. The mood of Depression causes the loss of appetite and an exhausted feeling. Humor blood takes over the Circulatory system, and this is where disease takes over. FEAR then is your constant companion.

QUESTION: Do you worry about your home, your family or your friends? ANSWER: I do much thinking, I guess you call it worrying! I worry about the safety of my family, about their health, and of course I worry about the financial conditions of the home. If anything should happen to my husband, I don't know what I would do. So I worry about these things until I cannot go to sleep until the wee hours of the morning. Then I am tired and weary when I need to get up and be about my house duties!

COMMENT: This type of person will worry about NOTHING. It is second nature to them. They feel sorry for themselves and want it to show upon their face for everyone to see. All this person wants is attention. They want PITY for their NATURAL RESPONSIBILI- TIES they call burdens. They have no faith in the family or home, and all decisions must be of their making. They call to the families' attention, that this is Love. This Love is measured only by the amount of worry that takes place.

Worry is a habit and it cannot provide nor prove any worth! It is worrying that brings these words in def- inite trouble to this type of person. To FRET, to BOTHER, and to HARASS, these actions are indeed destructive habits. When you FRET, you are showing FEAR. This is a disturbed mental condition. You try to build a wall or condition, that you call protection, about your family and yourself. Trouble has already entered in

130

when FEAR came. Calmness can do nothing, for if this person appeared calm, then no one would feel sorry for them and they would not attract attention. To BOTHER is their opportunity to get attention, so they talk to everyone and anyone they contact that will listen, and soon they find they are left much alone. To HARASS brings about a revengeful mental nature, it is vicious and cruel thinking, and this thinking takes place upon the body. Selfishness is present and shows to friends and family. This causes your imagination to form unreasonable opinions, and makes your world and surroundings a very unhappy, and unhealthy place to abide in.

QUESTION: Do you have undesirable habits? ANSWER: Yes, I do have some habits! I have been told some of these habits could be injurious to my health. I like to eat rich foods, and I drink, but not much, and I smoke. Most of my friends have these habits and when I am with them, I must be sociable.

COMMENT: These habits are weakness of character. As you are born free in this country, and old enough to think for yourself, you can make your own decisions. When you make these decisions, you must accept what develops from habit use. TO EAT RICH FOODS, will produce a sluggish body and mental mind. The nervous system is seeking a stimulant because the body is not getting sustenance to conduct the working of systems normally, to be natural. The vital organ of your body, the STOMACH, will form ULCERS. Drinking affects the LIVER, and ITS ACTIONS effect other vital organs. Smoking does affect the respiratory system, in this case, the LUNGS. Drinking can produce Cancer of the Liver, and smoking can produce Cancer of the Lungs. This is not all, your whole system or body will be contaminated with this dreadful, rotting disease. What is your gain that holds you spellbound to social standards? Is your social gain worth the price of unending suffering and pain? Take time out to do some thinking, be an independent person. Think for yourself, do not be persuaded by the social friends, who desire to lead you as long as you are useful for their good times. YOU BE THE LEADER, and show them good habits to follow. Learn that when you desire strength to say "NO", and mean it, friends will follow you, for you will be their leader. By helping yourself, you will be helping others to find health and great joy. May you consider well, that in your Bible, Jesus, CAST OUT THE EVIL SPIRIT, from a man who had come for a healing. What is an evil spirit? It is a departed earthling, who lives in Spiritland, and has found the way to attack persons on earth in the physical body. Yes, they do live after death. They attack those who have bad habits. There is much that can be told about evil spirits.

QUESTION: Do you feel that you are being blamed for things that go wrong or get out of order? ANSWER: Yes, I seem to get the blame for everything that goes wrong about the house. I have the feeling that my friends feel that I am wrong in what I say or do, most of the time. I feel that I do not get the attention I deserve from the family, or from my friends.

COMMENT: Here you can see the EMOTIONAL FEELINGS have taken over. This person desires sensational attention. They want words of praise and find they are not true many times. In their disappointment of the empty words, they form jealous thoughts, and they become selfish in their thinking and actions. Then loneliness takes possession of reasoning. They lack will power, the ability of doing right, and they appear to be clumsy in their actions, and so they do get the NOTICE, and the attention that at first seemed so important. This person will become fanatical, and soon will lack a mental balance, and in time will become insane.

EMOTIONAL FEELINGS leave an insecure attitude, and when the normal physical energies are depleted, the animal energies are drawn into the body to the lower nerve center. When this does happen, it works upon the NATURE PASSIONS. For example, sex activity, anger, temper, jealousy, and depression moods. Here is the time to turn to the many duties of a home, and be thankful for these duties, for then you will not be thinking of your EMOTIONAL FEELINGS. Keep cheerful when you are alone, and when you are with family and friends.

These words are for deep thinking. Read them, say them often, for they will help you to be the overcomer.

ADDENDUM ON THE RACES

The Masters presentation of the races has raised many questions in readers of the first edition of this book. We would like to offer a brief comment in this regard.

As we understand it, the ancient white race was the first race to have the Israel or light connection. Today there are Israel in every race, but not all of every race have taken on the Israel advancement as yet.

America was chosen long ago to be the new home of the advancing Israel, and the greatest concentration of the Israel on earth today dwell in America. This is the time chosen when many of the Israel will ascend and others are being prepared to be the future leaders of their race evolution.

Not one on earth is more important or more loved by God than another, but there are many stages of evolution in progress. We hope this will help to clear up some of the questions.

Seekers and Servers

ORDER FORM

To order extra copies of this book if they are not available in your bookstore *SEND CHECK OR MONEY ORDER MADE PAYABLE TO <u>SEEKERS AND SERVERS</u> ALONG WITH COMPLETED FORM TO:*

SEEKERS AND SERVERS
PO BOX 378
MT. SHASTA, CA 96067

MY MEETING WITH THE MASTERS ON MOUNT SHASTA

QUANTITY   PRICE

_____ X $7.95   = _____

CA RESIDENTS ADD 7.25% TAX + _____

TOTAL   = _____

SHIP TO: (PLEASE PRINT CLEARLY)

NAME _____

ADDRESS _____

CITY _____

STATE _____ ZIP CODE _____

☐ Please put me on your mailing list to receive notice when the next book is available.

Notes

Notes